Get Involved!

Making the Most
of Your 20s and 30s

By Tom Baker

ISBN: 978-0-615-18534-7

ATTENTION: Professional organizations, community groups, colleges and universities: Quantity discounts are available on bulk purchases of this book. The book can be customized to fit your specific needs. Contact us at 412-608-8842 for more information.

ACKNOWLEDGMENTS

My wife, Erin – for agreeing to be the love of my life on July 10, 2004 and for her constant encouragement.

My mom, Patty – for all of her amazing support and for believing that we could "change the world"

My dad, Dr. Tom Baker – for making the first 12 years of my life incredible and teaching me to be a lifelong learner

My step-dad, Phil – for having a place in his heart for one Republican and for always treating me like a son

The Luznars, The Johnsons, Missy, Pap-Pap and Jan-Ma – for always believing in me and making family occasions full of good food and great memories

All of my teachers, coaches, heroes, friends and mentors – for helping me to grow as a leader and person.

INTRODUCTION

My wife Erin and I were both very involved during our college years at Millersville University where I was honored to serve as student body president. Luckily, our friends also enjoyed joining organizations, sitting on committees, and assisting in managing campus events. Now, over five years since completing my undergraduate studies, it has become apparent that the love for making a difference that existed within many of my friends has disappeared. People who spent as much time in meetings as they did in the classroom are now working 9-5 in their professional life and are not getting entrenched in their communities. Where has their desire to make a difference gone?

Within this book you will read about a myriad of ways in which you can get involved and become more active. Endless opportunities await all college students, graduate students and young professionals. Often times young leaders are the missing backbone of organizations, committees and neighborhoods. As you continue growing as a professional, it is important to remember the simple pleasure you felt when you participated in your high school or college musical, the times when you were on the playing fields of a varsity or intramural sport, or during the times in which you served as president or committee chair. The lack of not being a student anymore does not mean that you are not able to do these same types of activities in your daily life. Your twenties and thirties can either be a time of growth when you develop consistently or a period of your life in which you stay in the status quo and just get through the day. I hope that by reading this book you are motivated and inspired to get more involved and start making a big difference.

This book will provide you with some good ideas of ways that you can expand your horizons and broaden your skill sets. It also includes concepts that will help you get better connected to leaders and agents of change in your community. Being involved and active makes my life worth living and I am so thankful for all of the amazing leadership opportunities that I have been entrusted with in both my professional and civic life. I wish you the same success and hope that you will share with me any good experiences on your part that come as a direct or even indirect result of reading this book. I really care about our generation of leaders and know that together we can and will change the world.

Failing Forward

As a candidate for the Pittsburgh Public School Board at the age of 25, I faced a tough task of unseating a hard-nosed incumbent. I remember campaigning and talking with voters about the upcoming election in the South Side of Pittsburgh on a spring day in 2005. The citizens told me that they would not vote for the Allegheny County Prothonatary Michael Lamb or City Councilman Bill Peduto for mayor because both men were far too young to serve in a leadership role. Lamb and Peduto were both in their early 40s at the time and had a significant amount of experience. I quickly realized I would probably not be securing their support. While voters will verbalize concern over electing young leaders, they often can change their mind when they get to the polls. Within eight months after that encounter, Pittsburgh welcomed a 26 year old mayor named Luke Ravenstahl after the untimely death of beloved Mayor Bob O'Connor. Ravenstahl was elected to a term in office of his own in November 2007.

If you are a big thinker and establish goals for yourself, it is important to remember that you are not always going to succeed. As an avid reader of "Campaigns and Elections Magazine," one of my favorite articles is "Failing Forward." It

3

discusses several elected officials and candidates who may have lost an election but improved their personal or professional profile as a result of offering themselves for service. Bill Clinton and George W. Bush both lost their first races for Congress as did former Pennsylvania Governor Dick Thornburgh. I often tell people that generally you need to lose in politics a few times before you start winning. In Pittsburgh, one of the up and coming political leaders is Dr. Patrick Dowd. Dowd lost his first race for State Representative but went on to defeat a tough incumbent for School Board in 2003 and an even more hard-nosed elected official for City Council in 2007. If we take away lessons and knowledge from our defeats in politics or in life we can use these experiences to help us the next time we jump back into the race.

As you read this book, please remember that no matter how smart, energetic, ambitious, articulate or well-intentioned you are, you will endure setbacks and failures during your attempts to make a difference. From time to time, you will be looked over to sit on a non-profit board, you might lose an election or your services might not be needed within a community organization. It is vital to not give up and to work even harder to ensure that you give yourself a fair chance to succeed in your next pursuit.

Getting Known as a Non-Profit Leader

Non-profit boards are always looking for fresh blood and future leaders to help guide their organizations. Too often it becomes difficult for graduate students and young professionals who are involved in college to make the natural transition to becoming part of local organizations. In college, events exist to encourage students to learn more about clubs and consider membership. These types of events

Thoughts for Leaders:

"A small group of thoughtful people could change the world. Indeed, it's the only thing that ever has."

Margaret Mead

are not as well noticed beyond college, but they do exist. Young professional groups work diligently to promote these opportunities and attempt to connect concerned and ambitious graduate students and young professionals with opportunities for growth. If you do not know what groups are located within your area, a simple internet search or conversation with co-workers may lead you to an organization that will help engage you in the community. Young professional groups are also a great way to make friends and expand your network.

The unfortunate misconception is that non-profit boards are filled with CEOs, presidents and other significant local figures. Another urban legend is that boards are only interested in lawyers and accountants. It is true that some boards are comprised of solely upper echelon executives and it is also true that lawyers and accountants are attractive candidates because of their skill base. However, you should not use these false assumptions as excuses not to seek out opportunities to serve on non-profit boards and their accompanying committees.

If you are not certain if you and a board would benefit both you and the group, offering to serve on a committee or with a special event is a great starting point. Committee membership is an effective way to demonstrate your commitment and passion for an organization and its mission. Getting to know the president of the board, other board members and the executive director of the organization also will enhance your opportunities within the organization. They are looking for leaders who will be able to give of their time and talent for years to come. They are looking for you!

All Politics are Local

Getting involved in the political process is a tremendous way to become active in your community. No matter what your political affiliation is, there are ample opportunities to build your network and become a change agent through politics and government. Political parties, campaign managers, candidates and elected officials are always in need of volunteers and donors. Since most college students, graduate students and young professionals are not able to become a political factor through monetary contributions, it is important to demonstrate loyalty, passion and commitment through utilization of your "sweat equity". Sweat equity is often described as the level of dedicated effort that a person or group put into a project, initiative or effort of any sort. Unlike financial resources, we never run out of the sweat equity that we are able to share with the groups and causes that we care about. I would encourage you to utilize all of your own sweat equity and make the most of the skills that you possess and the time that you are able to dedicate. Sweat equity is, often times, the most useful and attractive resource that resides within you as a volunteer or leader.

The Democratic and Republican parties have established organizations aimed at attracting young members and future leaders of their parties. Groups such as the College Republicans and College Democrats exist to engage students in campaigns and outreach efforts. These groups often meet on a regular basis and expose students to politics and leaders within the region in which the institution is located. For some students who will not remain in the community in which their college or university is located, being a member of these groups is a solid introductory experience. If a student intends on residing near their undergraduate institution following graduation, he or she can lay groundwork for future professional opportunities. Sometimes this can even be a starting point for future candidacies.

A continuation of these efforts is achieved by groups such as the Young Democrats (YD) or Young Republicans (YR). Unlike college organizations, these clubs meet and operate within each county in a state. Since members of the YRs or YDs are generally situated and plan on living in their region for a longer amount of time, the connections that are made through these groups can be even more significant. Friends and colleagues that you meet today as a member of these groups may be future members of Congress or leaders in your state. The person sitting next to you at these meetings or the person talking with you at a reception might even be President of the United States someday.

While political clubs and organizations marketed to college students and young professionals might have enjoyable components to them, it is important to treat these involvements with a sense of professionalism in the back of your mind. Politics can be a bloody game and it is probably better that your significant friendships and relationships not come as a result of your political network.   Make some great contacts and connections, but don't lose sight of your friends outside of politics.   As odd as it may sound, finding a good balance of your political and personal life is vital to succeeding in politics. Learn what opportunities are available locally to get in the arena politically soon, and maybe you'll be making decisions about policies and laws in the next few years.

Young Candidates Can Win

While young candidates generally face an uphill battle, we see success stories every year of candidates in their twenties who are elected to office. In 2005, college student Casey Durdines was elected Mayor of California, PA. When elected to serve, Durdines was entrusted with leading his community but could not legally drink an alcoholic beverage or rent a vehicle. 2006 saw a fresh crop of 20-something State Representatives elected to the Pennsylvania State House. Many of these newly elected officials ousted public servants who had served in

Thoughts for Leaders:

"I like thinking big. If you're going to be thinking, you might as well think big."

Donald Trump

leadership roles for decades. A few had even previously retained their seats for nearly the lifespan of their challengers.

Younger candidates bring a fresh perspective and often lack the political baggage that long-term officials possess. President Bill Clinton was elected as the attorney general of Arkansas at the age of 30 and was governor of his state in his early 30s; Bill Scranton became Pennsylvania's lieutenant governor at 32; Senator Evan Bayh was elected as Indiana's secretary of state at 31 and governor at 33; and the citizens of Cleveland trusted now Congressman Dennis Kucinich as their mayor when he was 31. Kucinich was often called the "Boy Mayor" during his tenure. Dennis O'Brien, the current Speaker of the Pennsylvania House of Representatives was first elected to the State House at the age of 23. A good friend of mine, Gerald McGrew has served as mayor of his hometown, Dravosburg, PA since he was in his mid-twenties. Another friend, Justin Lokay, became the youngest person ever elected to the East McKeesport Council when he was 22.

There is no reason why you should not consider yourself as a future elected office holder, candidate, campaign leader or party official. Beyond volunteering on campaigns, there are also other ways to get involved immediately. Running for a lower ballot office is a great way to start on your political journey. Depending on where you live, your committeeman or committeewoman seats might remain vacant. If you are a democrat living in a more conservative part of your state or a republican living in a liberal section, you may have more of a chance to obtain a leadership role and move up quickly. It is much easier to become a "big fish" in a "small pond" when less people are vying to serve in positions that may be of interest to you. When a party or organization is less established it also gives you an opportunity to be the voice of change or the person who helps move your group back to prosperity. By getting involved in local politics, it is much easier to see the direct impact you are making on your community.

Set Goals Constantly

By focusing on what you would like to achieve in the near and also not so near future, you will create a road map of the path you need to take to succeed and grow as a leader. Setting short-term goals can be especially useful as they often lay out a few specific steps and also enable you to feel a sense of accomplishment more abruptly and quickly. I encourage you to make a list of goals that you would like to achieve by the end of this year. Make sure to keep these goals in a safe place and refer back to them from time to time to assess your progress.

Laying out goals for the next few years can also be helpful. These goals will help motivate you and enable you to think big. I often think about the types of things that I hope to achieve in the next 3-5 years and find myself feeling more motivated and encouraged after jotting down a list of my hopes and dreams. Even if your goals seem too lofty or ambitious, always write them down. Goal-setting is a time for creativity and free thinking, not a time to be judgmental about your past successes or perceived shortcomings.

What are 4 things you would like to accomplish by the end of this year?

1._____

2._____

3._____

4._____

What are 4 things you would like to accomplish in the next 3-5 years?

1._____

2._____

3._____

4._____

After you write these goals down, start thinking about the specific things you will need to do to achieve them. Setting goals is great, but you must have a plan or framework set in place to follow through with them. If you know other people who have achieved what you are setting out to do, ask for their advice and counsel. By making others feel part of the process, you can assemble some great guides. It can never hurt to have too many people pulling for you. Please also feel free to email me your goals. I would love to see them and will sincerely think about what I can do to help you achieve them!

There Are Always Excuses

For the most part, you will always be a busier person tomorrow than you are today. Still, I hear so many people say that they will get more involved, join a club or obtain an advanced degree when their life calms down or when things get easier at work. As years go on, I continue to hear the same people using the same excuses. While being realistic and rational about the hours you have in a day is important, it is just as important not to hold yourself back.

As life goes on, you will generally receive more responsibility at work. You will also potentially get

Thoughts for Leaders:

"The reward for work well done is the opportunity to do more."

Dr. Jonas Salk

married and have a family, if you do not already have one. It amazes me to see married couples in which both partners have fantastic jobs, have kids and still somehow manage to have a social life and make a difference in their community. To me, that is the example of people who have been able to find balance and who are also not willing to make excuses when opportunities come knocking on their door.

One of my favorite phrases has always been that if you need to get something done, ask a busy person to do it. I could not agree with this notion more. Busy people always seem to be the ones who are able to tackle another project or task. They are also generally more willing to serve in these roles and manage events and initiatives. Do you want to be perceived by your classmates, colleagues or friends as a do-er or as a person who is too busy making excuses to get the job done?

Building Your Future Connections, Today

It is important to not burn bridges and to build as many positive relationships, both professionally and socially, as you feel comfortable with. You never know who could be your future boss or someone who will vouch for you during a job interview process. No matter what your status is within your educational or professional journey, it is always important to keep good contact with like-minded people who are doing the things you are doing or things that you would like to be doing. There are various ways to build your future connections immediately.

When I worked at Carnegie Mellon University's H. John Heinz III School of Public Policy and Management in Career Services, I often encouraged students to conduct informational interviews. These interviews are a great way to get to know someone who you would aspire to be like or hold a similar position as someday. People generally like to talk about themselves and share their professional journey, so you should be able to get 15-30 minutes on the calendar of someone who you respect or are curious about through these informational interviews. It is very important not to ask for a job or seem desperate in these meetings. Instead, you are building a professional friendship and maybe even triggering a relationship with a mentor for years to come.

Since you are asking for the meeting in this situation, it is important to prepare questions for the person about how they got to where they are, the types of things they do in their role and about tough situations that they have had to encounter in their work. It isn't a bad idea to have a copy of your resume on you for these sessions, but do not give them a copy unless it seems as if they want one. This person might be your boss someday or even recommend you to fill in for them when they move on or retire, so make sure to make a good impression and build a relationship that can benefit both of you in the future.

Business cards and contact information are important items to keep. Before attending an event, it is important to make sure that you have an ample supply of your own business cards with you. Also, when you are at an event, do not be scared to ask other people for a business card or present them with yours. This handoff can be, but certainly does not have to be, awkward or difficult. You do not want to stuff your card down the throat of a potential colleague or seem awkward in asking for his or hers.

Very often it is not what we know, but who we know, that helps us move forward professionally. Make sure to expand your network continuously and proactively network in a way that makes others think of you as a good possible colleague someday. The benefit of these efforts might not pay off immediately, but will over time. Get out there and get connected today!

The Youngest Person in the Room

Being the youngest person in the room is not such a bad thing. Do not avoid or look negatively at times in which you are the youngest person in the room at meetings or events. While this can be overwhelming from time to time, try to make the most out of these experiences. If you act professionally and politely, people will assume that you are older and more seasoned. It is fine

Thoughts for Leaders:

"If you don't know where you're going, you'll end up someplace else."

Yogi Berra

to keep people guessing about your age and surprise them by being younger than they had expected. In fact, it is a pretty fun feeling to keep others wondering.

Once you have completed either your undergraduate or graduate studies and enter the full-time working professional world, age matters less and less. I generally attend 2 to 3 meetings a day in which I am the youngest person in the room and have come to not even notice it anymore. It is natural to notice this at first, but it becomes increasingly comfortable as the years go by. As the youngest person in the room, it is important to be ready to speak on behalf of people in your age group. Providing a youthful perspective is a way for you to gain respect and also become a useful part of the conversation.

I often hear the phrase, "a seat at the table" used when talking about getting young professionals involved in important decision making processes. Make sure to thank those who help you "get a seat at the table" and be prepared to showcase why you deserve to be there. Come prepared to meetings and have specific ideas for improvement. Also, do not be afraid to sit back a little and observe the ways in which the movers and shakers communicate and get their points across. Being around accomplished people is a great way to learn and develop your own skills and learn new techniques.

As I have moved from my early twenties to my mid-twenties and now that I am in my late twenties, I relish the opportunity to be the youngest person in the room. In future decades, we will no longer get to be the fresh face in a meeting or at an event. Let's enjoy these experiences and the opportunity to serve as the youthful voice while we can.

Dress for Success

In the first five to ten years of your professional career, it is advisable to carefully consider what you will wear to networking events, meetings and other professional situations. In my own pursuits and when discussing attire with friends and colleagues, I generally think it is important to dress at a similar level, if not one notch above, the rest of the people with whom you will be interacting. It is generally easier to make your outfit less dressy if you have overshot when preparing for an event. If you are a man, you do not want to be the one person not wearing a tie and if you are a woman, it is not advantageous to be the only person not wearing a business suit. I generally keep an extra dress shirt and tie in my car just in case I need to change in the middle of the day. (I also am a bit of a messy eater so it can be helpful to have some extra clothing around.) Also, do not be afraid to ask your colleagues what they plan on wearing to an event that you are going to be attending. It might feel a little silly or childish the first time, but comparing notes on what your co-workers are wearing can help both of you.

Even though our culture generally motivates people to want to look younger, in your professional career it is to your benefit to keep people guessing or thinking that you are a few years older and more seasoned. I have spent much of my twenties having people guess or predict that I was in my thirties. This has never come across to me as offensive or rude. I appreciate the feedback and in a way am glad that they look at me as someone who is a bit more mature and professional. Dressing for success will enable you to build your reputation and come across as the emerging leader that you are. It will showcase to others that you take yourself and your career seriously.

Overcoming BMOC and BWOC Syndrome

I really loved my collegiate experience at Millersville University. I had an amazing group of friends and earned a good deal of respect as student body president and also president of my fraternity, Lambda Chi Alpha. Life was good and I assumed that the flattering feeling I had while in

Thoughts for Leaders:

"Leadership and learning are indispensable to each other."

John F. Kennedy

college would continue even after I earned my undergraduate degree. Like many others who I know were involved and "difference-makers" on their campuses, the real world can bring some harsh realities and can be quite humbling. For the people who were sometimes noted as being BMOCs (Big Men on Campus) or BWOCs (Big Women on Campus), moving beyond college can bring some tough realities.

27

As student body president, my thoughts and feelings on issues were often solicited and considered by the power-brokers at my college. Students who are involved also are able to turn large colleges and universities into more manageable and comfortable communities. Losing this can be tough at first. In many ways, you truly do need to start over and let go of that comfortable feeling that either your undergraduate or graduate institution has provided.

For the year following the completion of my college years at Millersville, I remained in Lancaster County as I waited for my then fiancé to complete her degree. My wife of three years now, Erin, was part of the class of 2003 while I completed my undergraduate experience in 2002. Staying in my college town was really tough for me and I found it difficult to move on. Also, we were planning to move to Pittsburgh in the fall of 2003, so I was much less inclined to get involved outside of work during that year. It took moving away from the area in which I attended college to start over and build a new, but equally satisfying and successful social and service oriented life.

To the Next Step

We always take our past experiences with us as we move from opportunity to opportunity. However, we cannot rely on our past achievements as a safety net that will guarantee future successes. As we move from high school to college and perhaps onto further education, it is important to come into each next step with a renewed sense of passion. The same holds true in the working world where you will encounter new co-workers as you move to each new professional opportunity.

While the skills and knowledge you have gained will not escape you, any reputation or respect that you received in the past will not automatically continue. You should come into each new experience with a passion to make a name for yourself, in a positive way, of course. While you want to seem prepared and ready to lead, it is vital not to overdo it in the first few weeks in a new role. I can think of people who seemed a little overeager to lead both in my educational and professional life and often times they fell out of favor with most people or burned out quickly.

People might be impressed with what you have done in the past. If that is the case, don't shy away from what you have achieved, but let others do the talking about these things. If someone asks you questions, tell them the truth. But, try not to go out of your way to brag about being valedictorian of your high school or a top scholar in your college or graduate school. It is really awkward when people constantly brag about themselves and generally, I think, people want to see or be part of your accomplishments. When the next step comes in your professional or educational journey, I would encourage you to consider what you bring to the table and then start moving full force to get known for the great things you are doing in your new environment. Your reputation is only as good as what you do today.

Opportunity Doesn't Always Knock at Your Door

As a student, no matter what level, the next chance to succeed and grow is generally searching for you. Your teachers, coaches, counselors and advisors usually serve as great advocates for you and will ensure that you are made aware of the next opportunity to apply for a scholarship, win an academic or service award, or serve in a leadership role. Even though these same types of mentors can and will exist in your professional life, they are not as plentiful and determined to help you succeed because they expect you to start taking responsibility.

The best opportunities that will come your way will most likely be the ones that you research or find on your own. Bouncing ideas off your friends and colleagues is important. If you are interested in a program or course that will help you develop, be sure to mention this to people within your network. Since good deeds often do, and always should, go both ways, make sure to be on the lookout for opportunities that will benefit everyone from your boss to someone who you run into at your local bar or gym. If you want others to help you, it is imperative for them to know that their best interest is also something that you are considering.

Service and fraternal organizations are a great way to make friends and also enable you to help your community. Having been a big greek life enthusiast in college, becoming a member of the Free and Accepted Masons was a natural fit for me. Being a member of this provides the sense of brotherhood and unique bond that I have always enjoyed about being part of fraternities. I would encourage you to take a look at what groups, lodges, and clubs exist close to you. Perhaps becoming involved in Rotary Club, Optimist Club, Kiwanis Club, Lions, Jaycees, Junior League, or the Knights of Columbus will align well with your interests and help you move forward as a community leader. If it makes sense for you at this point, being a member of your Chamber of Commerce can be beneficial. These groups all are a great place to promote your business or employer while making connections and building relationships. Most of these organizations are also in the market to recruit people in their twenties and thirties in an effort to help boost their membership and solidify their long term ability to stay relevant and functional. These groups want to get you active and involved with their efforts for many years to come.

One of my favorite quotes is from legendary baseball slugger, Babe Ruth. Ruth said, "Never let the fear of striking out get in your way." As you seek opportunities to grow and expand within your professional and social horizons, do

Thoughts for Leaders:

"Every new day begins with possibilities. It's up to us to fill it with the things that move us toward progress and peace."

Ronald Reagan

not be afraid that you will not be picked for a program or selected to serve on a board or committee. The more you persist and attempt to achieve, the more opportunities will start coming your way. Your first stages and initial attempts might be humbling, but eventually those great opportunities will start knocking at your door.

Working for Grades Might Be Over, but Keep Reading and Taking Classes

A nice thing about completing your school years is that the homework ends. I often speak with people who miss being in school in all ways except for the homework that accompanies our educational experiences. However, being out of school does not mean that learning and growth should conclude. In fact, some of my most enriching educational experiences have come from reading biographies and autobiographies in the time since I have completed graduate school. While books can be expensive, there are many websites that will enable you to purchase these items for a fraction of the cost.

I would encourage you to start building your own personal leadership and professional development library at your house or in your office. There is so much that we can take away from reading about leadership and management in these types of books. Some of my favorite leadership-focused authors include Stephen Covey, Jack Welch, Tony Robbins, Dale Carnegie and John Maxwell. If you have not read any of their books, I would definitely encourage you to track down some of their work. You will not be disappointed.

Completing one-day or semester-long trainings or courses is also a great way to continue growing. These opportunities certainly do not need to break your bank. If you have a community college nearby, it might prove advantageous to look through their course catalogue. Your local library or Chamber of Commerce might also offer these types of opportunities to learn more and develop new skills. We have a great program in Pittsburgh called The Leadership Academy which Is run through Duquesne University's Non Profit Leadership Institute. Other programs in my community include Leadership Pittsburgh, Inc. and also various programs through the Coro Center for Civic Leadership. A simple Google search or conversation with a friend or colleague could guide you to some of these amazing enrichment opportunities that exist close to you.

It is a small world, after all. This popular Disney phrase was often used by my graduate school professors as they worked to help my classmates grow into true professionals. As you move forward in your professional career, please keep in mind that other people are always watching you. I say this not to make you paranoid, but instead to alert you to the fact that behaviors

Thoughts for Leaders:

"You don't just luck into things. You build them step by step, whether it's friendships or opportunities."

Barbara Bush

that may have been perceived as laughable can be seen now as increasingly juvenile or immature.

Whether or not to drink alcohol at events or how much alcohol to consume at professional or community events can be a difficult decision to make. It is important to remember that the people you meet at these events could be your future mentors, supervisors or serve as useful connections. While it is beneficial to be seen as likeable, you do not want to get a reputation as a party animal. Excessive gossiping is also a negative behavior that many young professionals often get caught up in. While it might seem like you live in a big city or town, the working world breaks these communities down sector by sector. Being a big partier or someone who cannot be trusted with sensitive information are ways to become well known for all of the wrong reasons.

Stay Positive When Times Are Tough

I fail more often than 90% of people who I know. I have lost many elections; I am denied for numerous grants in my work; and I have been passed over for more than a hundred jobs. When I completed graduate school, I subsequently concluded my time as a career counselor at Carnegie Mellon University. I was being considered (and generally was passed over) for a number of positions. I was basically treading water and waiting to see what would happen. I was also sleeping until 11 a.m. and then going to the $1 Maxi Saver Movie Theater near our house. These were not the happiest times for me and are a great reminder that you are always better off looking for a job when you have a job.

Although failing during this time in my life was a bit upsetting, it truly humbled me and changed my outlook on some of the harsh realities of the working world. I never take having a job for granted anymore. We should enjoy the times in life when we are in good positions that stimulate us and help us grow. Too often we think these positions are a dime a dozen and endless jobs are waiting for us. Being unemployed, even for just a few weeks, taught me to be grateful for what I now have professionally.

An even more tear-jerking type of failure can be found through politics and elections. There is no feeling like losing an election, especially one that is covered by the local media. You start to think differently and find yourself giving the 60% of people who didn't vote for you a mean look at the grocery store. The experience of losing a race as a campaign manager is not a whole lot better. In my experience as a campaign manager, I found seeing people after the election loss to be very awkward. People generally assume that good people who stand for good things will win elections. This is definitely not the typical result. Politics might be the only business in which more than 50% of the people working hard to win will inevitably lose. In my experience, the key is to skip going to the grocery store for a week or so after the election, then proudly head back out with your head held high.

Dance with the Girl
Who Brought You

The circumstances and priorities within your life are always changing. As time goes on, it is important to treat your roots with honor. The best way to do this is by giving back to the groups, organizations and academic institutions that guided and developed you into the person you are today. Personally, I find it a bit odd when people try to completely distance themselves from the groups, schools or even occasionally the people who have helped mold them into the leaders they are today.

I would also encourage you to remain in contact with former classmates, friends from organizations and clubs and anyone with whom you enjoyed spending time during your high school and higher education years. It is not necessary to spend time with these people every day, but it is important to have a way to keep the lines of communication open. As technology grows and expands, this becomes easier and easier. I am amazed at how many people in their late 20s and 30s are on social networking sites like MySpace and Facebook. Heck, even my mom has a MySpace account that she checks every day!

If you are going to participate in these sites, I would just remind you to keep it professional. I even think of these sites as extensions of our website for work and my political website.

> **Thoughts for Leaders:**
>
> *"You cannot be a leader and ask other people to follow you, unless you know how to follow, too."*
>
> Sam Rayburn

Besides being a great way to extend friendships and keep in touch, these electronic mechanisms are also a great way to stick and linger in people's minds. However, you don't want to stand out in a negative way. Increasing numbers of employers are viewing these sites for background research on candidates. It is useful to think of these sites as extensions of your resume and, while it is fine to embrace your fun side on these, you should make sure that the content would be suitable to be viewed by a potential employer or supervisor.

Keep Minutes Today, Run Meetings Tomorrow

As you get more involved with organizations and boards, I recommend considering leadership positions as a way to enrich your experience. Getting elected as the secretary of an organization is not very difficult because the position is rarely desired. However, people do like to elect someone as president who has held an executive board position. As a fairly prolific secretary throughout my own leadership

Thoughts for Leaders:

"A community is like a ship; everyone ought to be prepared to take the helm."

Henrik Ibsen

experience, I have become a firm believer that with information comes a certain sense of power. Being secretary will enable you to organize the meeting minutes and sometimes you will even help develop the agenda or send out communication to your fellow members.

Your peers will also appreciate the work that you do as secretary because it is generally perceived as grunt work. I find that taking minutes is a great way to feel a part of the meeting and is a way to concentrate more. Perhaps most importantly, serving as secretary of an organization or board will give you access to and enable you to collaborate with either the chair or president of your group. This mentoring can be invaluable and when they are looking for a successor they will often think of you due to your commitment and dedication to the organization.

Planning Events is a Great Start

Events are a staple of just about every group in existence. Groups utilize events to raise funds, promote programs or just to meet socially. Serving on specific event committees is a great way to make a good name for yourself and show what you can do if given the opportunity. Events are enjoyable to be involved with for a number of reasons, including the sense of finality that

Thoughts for Leaders:

"Motivation is the art of getting people to do what you want them to do because they want to do it."

Dwight Eisenhower

they bring. When working on events, there is an end date in which it will be fairly obvious if the work you did led to a positive or negative experience for those in attendance.

I would challenge you to consider serving as a chair or co-chair of an event that you have enjoyed attending or have been minimally involved with. There are professional benefits and chances for advancement within an organization that can be a result of the good work you do in leading these events. I was given the opportunity to co-chair PUMP's Discover Pittsburgh in 2006 and 2007 and, luckily for me, I was positioned with two amazing co-chairs who worked tirelessly to make this large event a success. I am especially fond of my 2007 co-chair, my wife Erin. Just a few short months after Discover Pittsburgh 2007, I was elected to serve as the president of the board of directors for PUMP.

When considering future president or chair candidates, your peers will remember the good work you do in organizing programs and implementing plans along with your team. If nothing else, events are simply fun and will keep you looking forward to creating gatherings that you can be proud of helping to make possible.

To Do Lists

As your level of commitment continues to grow, I would highly recommend utilizing "To Do" lists to stay organized. I often see a small group of people crossing paths while serving in a diverse assortment of roles. Many of these "do-ers" often associate their success and ability to serve in various roles to their dedication to being organized professionals. The 80/20 rule holds true in every community in which I have been a part. Twenty percent of the people will most likely do 80% of the work and will wear many hats as leaders of several organizations and groups.

There are many ways to organize your life, but "To Do" lists seem to be a consistently productive habit. Jotting down the items that you would like to complete in a specific period of time will help you focus. It also provides a specific fall-back plan for times when you become distracted or lose momentum in your productivity level during the day. The feeling of highlighting items, putting a star next to them, striking a line through tasks or any recognition tactic that you choose is a good one. You can specifically see what you have completed and what still lies ahead for you. By being organized and utilizing a system such as "To Do" lists, you will be able to do more for your community and your company. "To Do" lists also help keep us away from the endless distractions that can arise during the work day. Whether it is chatting with co-workers, reading about current events on the web, or simply staring off into space, it is easy to lose focus. Having a "To Do" list by your side will help you stay productive and enable you to get more done during the work day and even on the weekend.

When in Doubt, Show Up

It is so easy to talk yourself out of trying something new. This sense of hesitance is no different for people who are considering attending their first meeting or event with a new organization. Truth be told, you will never have an exact sense of what to expect in a new situation. However, that in no way should serve as an excuse to stay at home and miss out on potential good opportunities to meet new people.

Thoughts for Leaders:

"You miss 100% of the shots you never take."

Wayne Gretzky

I am generally an outgoing person but can be a bit shy at first in new situations. Something that really helps me in new situations in which I know a limited amount of people is chatting with other people who don't seem to know many people either. Asking questions to the other person in this situation is generally a good first step. People generally like talking about their professional careers and that can be a good first topic to discuss. Talking about where they have attended school is also a pretty safe subject. Both of these topics certainly are more interesting than the other awkward topics of conversation, such as the weather. I would encourage you to bring business cards with you and expect to receive a few from your new contacts.

You may have a great time or you may have a forgettable experience. You may make great business contacts or you may share a few forgettable conversations with strangers. Either way, you won't be left guessing about what could have been and, more likely than not, you will have a good first experience with a new group and a fresh set of people.

Don't Lose Track of the People Who Pay Your Bills

It is very easy to get distracted and lose focus on work. We spend our young lives picturing the day in which we will have our first big job or nice office. Still, once we get to that point, it can be easy to occasionally feel a little under whelmed. I want you to get involved and make a difference in your community, but have to alert or remind you that it is imperative not to lose your job in the pursuit of joining organizations and becoming a civic leader.

I have always loved doing a lot of things outside of work. My civic, political and social commitments play a very important role in my life and often motivate me to get out of bed in the morning. It is the thought of running meetings, attending events or even playing softball or poker that often motivates me. However, I am very aware of the fact that I need to work my tail off within my professional career. In fact, it is the looming prospect of these other endeavors that motivates me to make the most of my time at the office.

If you want to do things outside of work, you will need to showcase to your supervisor and colleagues that you are a productive professional who is a dedicated member of the staff. Making your supervisor feel as though he or she is a part of your extra-curricular success is a good technique to receive some flexibility in the workplace. You certainly do not want to overextend their kindness and leniency, but if your boss feels as though your success is a result of their relationship with you and their role in your professional growth, they are much more inclined to allow you to spend work time on these pursuits. To ensure that it is a mutually beneficial partnership, it is important to have sincere interest in what your supervisor does outside of work. If he or she is involved in community service or other worthwhile initiatives, it is completely appropriate to ask questions and even help if it seems like a normal extension. If there comes a time when your boss expresses dissatisfaction in your other commitments, it is important to remain loyal and show that you are a team player with a good work-life balance.

You Don't Choose If You're A Role Model

Within the sports world there is much debate of whether athletes are role models. I think all young professionals should assume that they are role models. Being a project manager, lawyer, teacher, public relations specialist, banker or a

Thoughts for Leaders:

"Example is not the main thing influencing others. It is the only thing."

Albert Schweitzer

nurse might not feel the same as having millions of kids watching you shoot baskets, sing or act on television, but you need to remember that there are people who look up to you. These people could be co-workers, your customers, your neighbors or the people with whom you serve on committees or boards. Your boss could even consider you as a role model based on the way in which you lead and prove yourself within the workplace. You never know who is watching you to see what step you will take next or how you will handle a tough situation.

I have had the honor of being a Big Brother with Big Brothers and Big Sisters since August 2002 and could not express what a great experience it has been. I was working as the director of a child development center in Lancaster and had recently graduated from college when I was matched with my little brother, Preston. I was looking for a neat opportunity to try and make a difference in the life of a young person and, at first, viewed this experience as a way for me to help someone grow. I never considered what I would get out of it personally and, five years later, I can tell you that I think I have learned as much, if not more, from our friendship as Preston has.

I mention my relationship with Preston in this section because of an embarrassing occurrence that took place back in the winter of 2002. I am not one to break the law or get in trouble, but I did have a bad habit at restaurants of ordering water and drinking pop (or soda for the non-Pittsburgh readers out there) instead. One night when I dropped Preston off at his house, his mom mentioned to me that she was concerned that he had started stealing drinks when he went to fast food places. He was ordering water and drinking iced tea or Pepsi! I was horrified by this and had no idea that he might not only look up to me for the good things I was doing, but also for the not so good things I did as well. I can proudly say that I've never "stolen" pop from a fast food joint since the winter of 2002 and neither has Preston. Being a role model is something that you cannot just switch on and off. Start thinking about how your actions might affect others all the time, whether you are at work, leading a group, or off the clock having fun with your friends.

Get Your Foot in the Door

When I was offered a low-paying position with Carnegie Mellon University, I can vividly remember calling my grandmother, Missy, and asking for her advice about whether I should take the job or find something else to do while completing my graduate studies at Indiana University of Pennsylvania. A lifelong Pittsburgh native, Missy's response was simple, but the passion behind her response surprised me a bit. She said, "Even if you have to pay them to work there, take the job. Being able to say that you worked at Carnegie Mellon is something that will benefit you for the rest of your life." While your circumstances might be different, I think Missy painted an important picture. Sometimes getting your foot in the door is really the key to becoming successful.

It can also be worthwhile to take less glamorous jobs with companies or businesses that you feel strongly about. In my time working in four different career services offices, I have always encouraged students to find a company or cause that they are passionate about and then work as hard as possible to get their feet in the door. It is often much easier to move up once you are employed by a company. But, finding employment with your dream organization is not always a simple task to undertake. Even when you seem like the perfect fit for a position, often times the job will be offered to someone else. This is not intended to discourage you. Instead, it is simply the law of averages that exists in the working world. When the chance comes to become part of a proven winner that you believe in, I would encourage you to worry less about title and salary and more about the long-term benefits of getting on board with something that could potentially positively affect your life for decades.

Work Like You Have
Your Ideal Job Title

Most people believe that job titles are important and I would be lying if I said that I did not believe this as well. However, I do not believe that your title is your identity. If you are unhappy with your job title, it is up to you, and you alone, to remedy the situation. Do not wait for your supervisor to charge you with completing the kind of tasks that you would like to complete. If you want to succeed, you need to act as if you have the job title you would have ideally. If you would like to be a manager or director, behave and work with the same intensity of those who hold those jobs.

The only time in my career when I did not manage anything at first was when I started at Carnegie Mellon. I was a career counselor there and was pretty much the low person on the office depth chart. No one reported to me and I was originally given minimal responsibility. By the time I left the position, I had organized and distributed a weekly electronic newsletter called eClips for two years, led our student organization in raising $30,000 for unpaid and low paying internships and critiqued over 500 resumes. I am proud to say that in September 2007, the 200th edition of eClips was distributed to the students, staff and alumni of The Heinz School at Carnegie Mellon University.

Becoming a club advisor in this position, I felt some of my leadership skills were being utilized

Thoughts for Leaders:

"There are no secrets to success; don't waste time looking for them. Success is the result of perfection, hard work, learning from failure, loyalty to those for whom you work, and persistence."

Colin Powell

and enjoyed supervising our student volunteers. More importantly, in my office I positioned myself as the number two person for my boss. Whatever he needed, I did. If it meant meeting with important employers, filling in for him in meetings with students or even setting up the pizza and pop for seminars, I gladly did it all. Through this, I learned what it was like to manage a career services office, gained a ton of institutional knowledge, and earned a reputation as someone who could get things done and was willing to be a leader. If you feel unhappy with your current role, think about ways in which you could take more responsibility and display the tremendous strengths that you hold inside.

Build Memories, Build Tradition, Build Pride

You might be thinking to yourself that this section sounds like a cheesy student council campaign slogan. If so, you are absolutely correct. "Build Memories, Build Tradition, Build Pride" was our campaign theme when I ran with four of my friends for student government executive board at Millersville University back in 1999. Speaking of cheesy, our campaign team was called "The Fab Five", largely due to me being a big Michigan basketball fan in the early 1990s. Michigan's Fab Five, which consisted of Chris Webber, Juwan Howard, Jalen Rose, Ray Jackson and Jimmy King, are a legendary group of teammates who transcended college basketball in the early 1990s. They participated in the national championship in consecutive years and made a splash by wearing baggy shorts and changing the way basketball was played. The amazing thing about the Fab Five was that all five of them were starters as freshmen when they advanced during the March Madness tournament in 1992. I was a big fan of the Fab Five and thought it would be a neat name for the group of five sophomores that I had assembled to run together for the five officer positions at Millersville University. Like Michigan's Fab Five, we ended up doing well and went on to make a big difference on Millersville's campus.

Assembling a great team to work with you when you are considering running for president or chair of any group is vital if you want to get elected and, more importantly, lead effectively. I enjoyed two great years as student body president because of the Fab Five. Whether it is the people working most closely to you or less involved members of a group, I think it holds true that people generally want to be inspired. People don't elect you or choose you to serve in a role because they want you to be negative. They want you to succeed while increasing the enthusiasm and morale of the organization. The Fab Five started a full day of activities and events called "MU Pride Day" and a series of discussions focused on bringing people together, "Dialogue on Race". When I was president of our graduate student organization, Associates for Student Development, we created a student-run journal called The SAHE Review and developed a Leadership and Professional Development Library. Special projects and initiatives were always something that I enjoyed doing in college and graduate school and still do in my professional and civic life. If you like starting new programs or have ideas in your mind, be sure to share them with others and help lead your group in getting them implemented.

For groups to prosper, it takes a good deal of work. As you move forward, I would encourage you to be the person who brings people together, organizes social get-togethers or even takes pictures at events. My wife thinks I am a pack rat, but I honestly enjoy keeping a record of what happens by capturing photos and keeping items. Your peers will appreciate these habits in you, in part because they may not want to do it themselves. Some people are too shy to plan a group outing or not outgoing enough to ask someone to take a picture of your group. I know these things seem basic, but they are often overlooked. Make a point to do the little things to increase the memories that are created, the traditions that are organized and the pride that is felt within your group.

All in the Family

If you are looking over options and brainstorming ideas as you decipher what might be a good fit for your involvement, the answer might be sitting next to you at the Thanksgiving dinner table. My parents were both educators who cared deeply about improving the lives of students. My father, Dr. Tom Baker, taught in the Pittsburgh Public Schools throughout his entire professional career. He was my first hero and role model. What I found especially interesting about my dad was his interest in doing things outside of work. He was an author and wrote a series of books for high school students with lower reading skills. He also was named Coach of the Year for my little league, was the editor of the school district newsletter and even was the mascot (Owlbert Einstein) of the Pittsburgh Public Schools. Much of my childhood was spent going from community event to community event watching him as he made his best effort to make a difference. My father lost his battle with cancer at the age of 39 in the early 1990s and I can't even imagine what he would have done in the last 16 years.

My mom, Patty Baker (now Verostko) was no slouch either. My mom was a teacher before she decided to stay home in the early 1980s to raise me. When I was young, she always had interesting jobs and really connected with people while working in a clothing store, gift shop and pharmacy. She also was really interested in educational issues and got involved in PTO and through my clubs and organizations. When my dad passed away, my mom stepped up to the plate, almost literally, and started coaching little league and pony league. Having a mom as a little league and pony league coach wasn't a common occurrence, but she did an amazing job in the role. Both of my parents were the "coolest" coaches around and favorites of my teammates. Since she got remarried to my stepfather Phil in 1997, my mom has jumped back into the educational community, working for organizations like Head Start and United Cerebral Palsy.

The purpose of this section is not to simply tell you how proud I am to have been born to two wonderful people, but to remind you not to shy away from your parents' involvements. If there is something that one of your parents or family members has done, there is nothing wrong with taking a look at it or asking them how they got involved with a group or how they expressed their passion for a subject. While very few teenagers want to be like their parents, I have found that many 20 and 30 somethings end up not minding too much regarding the similarities and parallels that exist between them and their loved ones.

Loyalty Matters

When I was in high school, my mom used to always tell me how happy she was that I had good friends who had a positive impact on me. I am proud to say that I have been blessed with amazing friends throughout my life. In no way do I deserve the loyalty and passion that they have expressed and displayed for my interests and pursuits. Being loyal in return to your friends is such an important thing to do. Disregarding the feelings of your friends too often leads to the unfortunate conclusion of relationships.

I have always thought that it is important to tell someone if you appreciate him or her. But, I don't mean this in a fake way just so they will continue to do you favors. A great way to show friends that you care is to ask them about what is going on in their lives and to get involved in some of the things that they enjoy doing. Erin and I are very close to a married couple in Pittsburgh, Jeremy and Joyce. Joyce is a physician and Jeremy is a marketing manager at a local theater. Minus my somewhat comical role in "The King and I" in high school, Erin and I could not be a whole lot less artistic. I have always enjoyed television and movies, but never really had an interest in the stage. Jeremy started bringing us to events at his theatre and eventually asked us to serve on a young professionals group called "The Greenroom". I am told that the greenroom is the place where actors and actresses get ready for a show and was selected as our committee's name because we are preparing to help lead the theatre. This initiative has been an amazing success and we have been able to stand by our close friend during some of his most important professional accomplishments by being a part of this group. We are genuinely thrilled to do what we can to help him and the theatre and see them succeed.

Friends are an amazing place to get real and honest advice. You can feel much more at ease bouncing professional ideas off them and getting their feedback with regard to the decisions you are making inside and outside of work. When they ask you for counsel in similar situations, it is vital that you really think about what they are asking and give them useful and truthful advice. My friends always have and continue to motivate me to make a difference and follow my dreams. I would encourage you to share your hopes and wishes with those people whom you care about and who care about you.

Life Without Blind Resume Drops

My wife and I have experienced one main difference in our professional lives. I have been rejected for over 100 jobs and she has been turned down for less than five. Erin is a terrific networker and has done an amazing job at using this skill to find positions that appeal to her. She is currently working for one of the largest employers in our region, earning an amazing opportunity through persistence and using her network. She got to know her current supervisor while in her previous position and was able to showcase how talented and dedicated she was. When it took

Thoughts for Leaders:

"I am a great believer in luck, and I find the harder I work, the more I have of it."

Thomas Jefferson

an extra five months for her new company to finalize her position and get approval, she remained patient and kept a cordial relationship with him. Erin is now in her dream job because of the way she utilized her network. She is a great example for all of us, including me!

The connections you make through networking can often times become a great reference for a future job or even a future boss. Nepotism is an ugly practice that can plague business corporations and government. Still, the truth is that it often matters just as much what you know or the skills that you bring the table as it does who you know. People like to hire people that they feel as if they can trust and often do not want to take a chance on someone who could be perceived as a wildcard.

A nice thing about being a solid networker is that your need to drop your resume blindly for positions will be greatly reduced. By building a solid base of colleagues and contacts, great opportunities will come your way and you will be able to avoid sending applications to people you do not know and receiving a form rejection letter for a job that you feel would be a perfect fit for you. Approaching every contact as someone who might, but doesn't necessarily have to, benefit your career will make a good impression while laying the groundwork for a prosperous future.

If You Don't Golf, Be Flexible

As you attempt to move your own career forward and aid the causes that you care about, it will become abundantly clear that you will be able to try new things. Much of what is accomplished in business and life is not solely completed in meetings. One of the more commonly known "outside of meetings" activities is golf. However, I am not a golfer and somehow have escaped to this point in my life without learning how to play. I think part of this is because I am flexible and attempt to make connections and build partnerships through other involvements and in other environments.

If you are looking to raise money for a board or committee that you work with or are trying to close a business deal, you can invite people out to lunch. Lunch is a safe activity because it generally has a clear start and end point. It also provides a great chance to really talk about the specific reasons why you had hoped to schedule time with this person. Another great way to network with a colleague is to invite them to join you at a sporting event or in a more social situation. When a colleague starts thinking of you as a friend the likelihood increases that they will at least try to make things work well for both you and the group that you are representing.

Not golfing might also lead to trying out some things you never thought you would like. As long as you feel comfortable trying the activity, I would strongly encourage you to attempt to participate in activities with your colleagues. The people that we have met through the Pittsburgh Sports League have been incredibly helpful to Erin and me. While we might not create partnerships or get sponsorships on the golf course, it is quite common for us to work jointly with the people that we play softball, basketball, soccer, and even bowl with through the Pittsburgh Sports League.

Cleaning Up Your Streets

The concept of thinking globally and acting locally is one that I think can be effectively utilized by young professionals. While it is very important to care about national and international issues and concerns, it is far much easier to make an immediate impact if you donate your time and talent to your local community. Taking a sincere interest in the well-being of your community is a great way to spend your free time and directly affects the people who live near you. Most neighborhoods have either community development corporations or non-profit organizations that strive to make improvements in their areas. They do this through holding community socials, organizing community service events and serving as the voice of the neighborhood in which we all live.

Erin and I live in a house across the street from where I grew up in a neighborhood in Pittsburgh called Greenfield. Within our community, we have a non-profit group named the Greenfield Organization (GO). The GO produces The Greenfield Grapevine, a community newspaper which promotes events, includes interesting relevant articles and gives updates on what community members are doing. Other initiatives that the GO works on are planning events like The Greenfield Glide (a large 5K race), night at the races, bingo nights and other events for seniors and local residents to enjoy. I was elected to serve on the GO Board for two years and enjoyed my time working with local community activists and organizers. The board even authorized me to co-chair The GO Hoops Classic, a basketball tournament for kids.

There is a growing number of young professionals in Greenfield, many of whom did not believe that

Thoughts for Leaders:

"Only a life lived for others is a life worthwhile."

Albert Einstein

the GO was addressing their interests. A steering committee of local residents came up with the idea of Connect Greenfield. Since it began, Connect Greenfield has already secured funding for a community mural, organized a block by block cleanup program and held several meet your neighbor nights.

I would encourage you to look into the organizations that currently exist within your community and at least check out their website or give their office a call to see how you can get involved. If nothing exists or you find that your local group does not address the needs of local residents, I would suggest that you gather your neighbors and friends together to see if something should be created to help make a difference on your local streets. It might sound better to join large scale groups, but you can have a direct impact on your neighborhood by getting involved locally.

Jogging at 8:30 a.m. on Saturdays

Being a good citizen often means participating in events. Some of these events will feel very normal to you while others might take some extra effort. I am always impressed to see the massive amounts of people who participate in 5K (3.1 miles) races, charity walks, bowl-a-thons, and other gatherings to support a specific cause. These events are generally fun and also help important organizations and groups raise money to directly aid people and causes.

The thought of running 3.1 miles on a Saturday or Sunday morning is not something that typically makes most people very happy. We work hard during the week and often times want to at least sleep in on the weekends. From experience I can tell you that if you haven't run one yet, you will appreciate running between 8 and 9 a.m. instead of the middle of the day when it is much hotter outside. I have always liked the intangibles about these events. Seeing lots of people out doing something healthy and supporting an important cause really motivates me to run harder. It is also a neat way to visit communities that you are not familiar with and maybe even meet some new friends. 5Ks certainly are just one example of charity events that are enjoyable to experience. There are many other similar types of events. I would encourage you to take a look in your local newspaper and see what community events and fundraisers are approaching. Then, set a goal to at least sign up for one race, walk or other fundraising initiative occurring close to you in the next few weeks.

The other side of these events is that you will continue to be asked to support your friends when they are taking part in fundraisers. Every donation makes an impact and your friends will appreciate the fact that you are willing to be part of their "team". Even if it is a modest donation, I would challenge you to try and give something to support these causes. I have been a co-captain for the American Cancer Society's Relay for Life three times and always learn so much through the process and event. It inspires me to see all of those dedicated people who care enough to walk laps around a track at 4 a.m., regardless of the weather, because they care about someone who has had cancer or are walking in memory of a loved one. The people who organize and give their "sweat equity" to raise money for important causes are definitely heroes in my eyes.

Keep Up On Current Events

When I was young I thought keeping up on current events meant reading the sports section in the newspaper everyday. Thankfully my

Thoughts for Leaders:

"If you are bored with life, if you don't get up every morning with a burning desire to do things – you don't have enough goals."

Lou Holtz

passion for knowledge has grown over the years and I, like many, enjoy reading and learning about current events through a number of newspapers and increasingly electronic tools. I would encourage you to keep an eye out for what is happening around you because it will generally either benefit you or allow you to assist others. Knowing what is going on will allow you to network more effectively and will demonstrate at least some passion or commitment to your community or region. Plus, nothing is worse than talking about the weather for ten minutes when you meet somebody for the first time. In taking stock of what is happening around you, it will also become increasingly easier to make plans to attend events, forums, debates, seminars and other useful growth or leisure opportunities.

There are so many ways to find out about events that I do not have a whole lot of sympathy for people who say that they never heard of something. While a sense of responsibility obviously falls on the staff or volunteers who are marketing an event, it is also your duty to attempt to learn about what is scheduled to occur in upcoming weeks and months. Signing up for email distribution lists and visiting websites on which you have found past opportunities are good ways to keep yourself informed. Being interested in these activities is a characteristic that others will find attractive in you. It will also enable you to learn more with regards to what you are passionate about and interested in.

Don't Lose Your Cool on Frustrating Days

It takes hard work and commitment to build a reputation of being a strong leader and genuinely good person. Unfortunately, it can take so much less time to lose that reputation with one misstep or outburst. I know a lot of passionate people and have witnessed some disappointing meltdowns in my career. When you feel yourself getting upset or agitated, I would recommend saying very little or removing yourself from a potentially bad situation. Too many good people throw away the hard work that they have done throughout their careers and through service work during these episodes.

Sitting on a number of non-profit boards has led me to participate in a fair share of three and four hour long meetings. I genuinely enjoy meetings, but even I can get really frustrated in that third or fourth hour. It is really tempting to say what you really think in these situations, but I would advise you to keep your cool and focus on the positive things that have been accomplished during the session. In times where I might say something harsh or call out somebody else, I will often send them an email or give them a call and either apologize or explain my rationale within the next

24 hours. This personal follow-up can go a long way with your peers and enables them to see things through your eyes a bit. In your attempts to make a difference, you will get frustrated. Still, try to focus on building a reputation around the quality of your work and not that one time that you yelled or screamed at a meeting or event.

If Money Didn't Matter, What Would You Do?

Working for a terrific non-profit organization allows me the chance to make a difference in the lives of teenagers and directly impact the communities in which we serve. Having said that, I am human and I do notice the amazing salaries of some of my good friends and colleagues who work in the corporate world. One common theme I have noticed from them is that they do not seem all that passionate about what they do and often times are not able to determine what they want to do on the side. When they ask me for ideas, I often tell them to think about what they would do for a living if money didn't matter. If they could make the same significant salary doing any job, what would it be?

If you are looking for something to do outside of work or school, I think this is a great question to consider. Depending on your answer and thoughts, you will be able to find groups and organizations that are addressing these issues and needs. If you feel strongly about empowering students to succeed, serving as a mentor would be a good fit for you. Those who care about animals might want to consider helping out a local facility or sitting on a committee or board for local animal groups.

Personally, I care a great deal about the region in which I live and think that it is important to attract and retain young professionals and

Thoughts for Leaders:

"If you want to be happy, set a goal that commands your thoughts, liberates your energy, and inspires your hopes."

Andrew Carnegie

college students in Pittsburgh. Due to that, I have really enjoyed my time serving on the board of directors of the Pittsburgh Urban Magnet Project (PUMP). The mission of PUMP is to advance issues effecting young and young-thinking people in Pittsburgh, making the region a more dynamic, engaging and diverse place in which to live. My passion for connecting people and providing them with amazing opportunities is embraced by PUMP's mission and it makes the hours that we spend in meetings and working on initiatives seem to go by quickly. Being part of PUMP and, more recently, serving as president of the board, has motivated me to work harder in all that I do to help this region grow and develop. I would encourage you to find a group that inspires and motivates you in a similar fashion.

From the Baseball Diamond to the Board Room

I weigh over 200 pounds and know that anytime a pretty big guy gives advice about being healthy, it probably comes across as a little odd. In no way do I intend to lecture you about your eating habits or fitness routine. I do want to mention two reasons why I think engaging in sports and working out consistently will make you a better leader and enable you to do more for your community.

First, getting a good workout does a lot of good for you in releasing stress and frustration. Sometimes before a long day or in between meetings, I will jump on our treadmill at home to let go of some of my excess energy. Running is also a great time to brainstorm and gather your thoughts. My wife is a very balanced person and is great at her job. I think part of this has to do with the fact that she works out for at least 30 minutes on our treadmill every morning. It really seems to set a great tone for the day. While the health-related reasons for exercising are fairly obvious, I think that the role that it can play in your outlook and attitude is almost equally important.

Also, there is much to be learned from participating in team sports. I have enjoyed team sports since I was eight years old and have taken so much away from these experiences. I have no doubt that being a leader on my baseball teams growing up has helped me to be a better student body president at Millersville University and that my current experiences with being a softball team captain within the Pittsburgh Sports League has enabled me to motivate and organize more effectively at work and in my other commitments. Sports have always been fascinating to me and I love caring so much about something that really doesn't change anything at the end of the day. That is partially what makes participating in sports so much fun. Sports are also a great place to expand your network and learn about the interests and pursuits of a diverse assortment of people that you otherwise might not know. If you are not engaged in sporting activities, take a look around and see what opportunities exist in your area. There is a great likelihood that you will feel better about yourself, make some new friends and release some stress through having sports as a part of your life.

More Than Just Acronyms on Your Resume

When I was in graduate school, I came to the realization that there are massive amounts of organizations with catchy acronyms. In my program most people were part of the larger student affairs organizations like ACPA (American College Personnel Association), PCPA (Pennsylvania College Personnel Association) and NASPA (National Association of Student Personnel Administrators). Some of my colleagues also were part of specialized organizations which focused on the specific functional area in which they worked or where they were interested in working.

Most professions have organizations that focus on the needs, interests and well-being of their members. I would encourage you to examine what national and also local organizations are currently in existence for your professional focus. Many of these groups hold excellent conferences, seminars and networking events. These are a great place to bounce ideas off people and learn about best practices that are being implemented in other parts of your state and throughout the country. Also, if the opportunity is available to give a presentation at the conference, make sure to consider what you could share that would be useful to other conference attendees. This is a great way to showcase your ideas and skills as a professional while making the most of the time that you are spending at the conference.

If you run into someone at these conferences who holds the position that you would love to

Thoughts for Leaders:

"Leaders need to be optimists. Their vision is beyond the present."

Rudy Giuliani

have someday, talk to them. They will be flattered that you are interested in learning about their career, priorities and goals. While conferences organized by professional organizations can be a lot of fun to attend, I believe that the real value is what you learn and who you meet. When you are at the conference, think about what committees are in place and if you would be interested in being a part of one, or even a few. I have always found working with people on committees and in planning events as a useful mechanism to make contacts and connections. Instead of focusing on fun, focus on the future while experiencing these potentially career-altering opportunities.

People Will Benefit from Your Guidance

When we think about who made a big difference in our lives during our younger years, the two largest groups that are often cited are either parents or teachers. While both our family members and teachers are very important, there are often other advisors and mentors who influence us in a positive way. I would ask you to take a moment to think about who these people were in your own life. If you haven't talked with them recently, pick up the phone or send them an email and thank them for the big role they played in your life. I can guarantee that your message will make their day and remind them of why they give their time in a selfless manner to work with youngsters in their community.

There are endless ways in which you can mentor students of all ages. My experience as a Big Brother with Big Brothers Big Sisters has been one of the best things I have ever done in my life. I would recommend this organization whole-heartedly to anyone who has an interest in directly impacting a young man or woman. My little brother, Preston, and I were matched in late summer 2002. We became good friends immediately and spent at least one evening a week together while I was still living in Lancaster, PA. When my wife and I moved to Pittsburgh in August 2003, Preston and I decided to maintain our relationship and are still very close after five years of being big and little brother. He makes me want to be a better person and inspires me to stay motivated and active. I hope that I have helped him during his teen years and know that we will remain close forever.

There are endless ways to become a mentor. Coaching a sport or serving as an advisor to clubs and organizations at an elementary school, middle school, high school or local college will allow you to have a direct impact on students. Many religious institutions have the ability for mentoring or educating younger students as well. Being a troop leader for the Boy Scouts or Girl Scouts is also a nice option for empowering young leaders. To be a mentor, you need to have an enthusiasm for the role that you are undertaking. Since you will be giving of both your "sweat equity" and usually some of your financial resources, it is important that you are ready to truly dedicate yourself to these opportunities. If you're not certain what mentoring opportunity is best for you, I would recommend talking to the people closest to you and asking them what they think would be a good fit.

Another good brainstorming technique is jotting down a list of experiences that were beneficial to you and think about becoming an advisor to that club, group, team or organization. There are so many students who are waiting for a mentor to become a part of their lives and to help them grow and develop. Do not waste any more time and be sure to formulate a plan today to serve in a mentoring role sometime very soon.

Shopping for Hobbies

Certain luxuries do not always continue to exist after you have left your school years behind. Still, our desire to be entertained and involved does not end simply because we are no longer students. If you are not doing much beyond work, I would encourage you to take a look at what opportunities are available in your town. Hobbies can be as involved as playing an instrument or competing on a recreational sports team, or as relaxed as reading books or following current events online. No matter what you do outside of work, having something going on is

Thoughts for Leaders:

"What we do during our working hours determines what we have; what we do during our leisure hours determines who we are."

George Eastman

important. If you are following American Idol, Dancing with the Stars or the football playoffs, having these outside interests will give you something to look forward to and also be a topic to discuss with friends and colleagues. Being passionate about something, no matter how obscure or seemingly "un-cool" it is, really will have a good impact on your life and your ability to connect with others. Having these interests can also become a valuable piece of your networking arsenal.

I have always been a big believer that there is something therapeutic and healthy in caring deeply about something that really doesn't affect your work. Football, baseball and basketball games do nothing for me professionally. Yet, I spend several hours a week watching teams compete, studying individual statistics and reading about players. In no way do I consider this a bad investment because it makes life more interesting. Sports also can make you feel as though you are part of a community, help you make friends and give you a sense of belonging. With increased technological advances, we continue to see more small communities developed online regarding many different subject areas, including sports. There are fantasy leagues, blogs, fan websites and various other ways to communicate your thoughts and beliefs regarding recent sporting events and occurrences.

When you talk to your friends, colleagues and new acquaintances, tell them about what sparks your interest and make sure to listen when they return the favor and discuss their passions with you. If we spent a day together, you would undoubtedly hear me talk about some of my favorite television shows, movies, musical artists, sports teams and athletes. In return, I would plan to hear about what you are involved and absorbed in outside of work. When people tell you what they are interested in, make a point to remember so that you can continue the discussion the next time you see them. Whether it's a couple who scrapbook together, people taking yoga classes, or fans of music attending concerts, I think there is something so refreshing about the hobbies and interests that we pursue outside of our professional worlds. I heard a great quote at a Highmark Healthy 5 program that I think sums the need for hobbies appropriately. "You don't stop playing because you grow old; you grow old because you stop playing!"

If You Don't Have Money, Give Your Sweat Equity

The concept of loving what you do seems so basic and simple. However, I cannot tell you how many people I know who either have a job or are involved in many groups that do not inspire and motive them. When you are doing something that you truly care about, the sweat equity that you will give will seem virtually effortless. Participating in early morning and late evening meetings are so much more pleasant when you are working on something that inspires you. Too often people are scared away from finding these enriching opportunities to give back because they assume that groups have mandatory annual donation requirements. There are so many ways to give back and make a difference without breaking your personal bank account.

While purchasing tickets to important events and fundraisers can be very expensive, taking advantage of volunteer opportunities is a free way to be helpful and still get to be part of these functions. By volunteering you also are assisting the organizers of the event in making it more efficient and effective for attendees. In my eyes, volunteering at events is a win-win scenario.

While serving on boards can be an expensive undertaking, it does not have to be. In recent years, I have had the pleasure to serve on five non-profit boards and when I am being considered for board service, I simply ask what the annual commitment is, if any. Unless there is a specific amount associated with a board, the standard answer is pretty simple. All board members are expected to make a significant donation that makes sense based on their financial situation. It is important for organizations to have 100% of their board giving. Board presidents and executive directors are often charged with the task of ensuring that all members have donated something during the current year. My personal decision in the past has been to shy away from groups who asked for a specific annual contribution, be it $500, $1000 or even higher. I prefer to give through my hard work, dedication and ideas. All of these types of support are part of the one resource that we have endless amounts of: our sweat equity.

Market Yourself

As you continue to make a difference in your community, I would encourage you to market yourself and what your group is achieving. Assume that you are the top executive in your own personal public relations firm and remind yourself that if you do not share your message, it will probably not get out there. One way to get

> **Thoughts for Leaders:**
>
> *"To avoid criticism, do nothing, say nothing, be nothing."*
>
> Elbert Hubbard

your name out there is by sending brief updates to the alumni newsletters and magazines from educational institutions that you have attended. Also, think about sending small "blurbs" to the newspaper in your neighborhood. I have generally found that more grassroots media outlets with smaller staffs are generally willing to help promote events and accomplishments of local citizens. By providing them with potential content, you are helping to enrich and broaden their news outlet. Bigger newspapers and magazines also offer updates about events and achievements. While it might be a little more difficult to lock down this type of "earned media", I would still suggest that you send your materials to them. It is incredibly important to be polite with the media and provide them with the information important to them. You want to help them as much as possible to ensure that you get the exposure you are seeking.

We live in a fast-moving world in which great opportunities can come your way when you least expect them. I would recommend having all of your job-related materials updated and ready to be sent to a colleague quickly if it is requested. I would recommend that you spend a few minutes every month reviewing your resume and seeing if anything could be added to strengthen or adapt it. In saying this, I am not suggesting that you should always be on the lookout for a new job. Often times when you are being considered for a non-profit board or committee service, you will be asked to submit a resume and, potentially, references or a cover letter. Having your professional materials updated will enable you to do this more promptly and also will ensure that the initiatives you have undertaken in recent months make their way into your resume. No matter how great of a person you are or how much you accomplish, your ability to try new things and excel will greatly rely on your ability to market what you have done. These tasks might seem anywhere from tedious to cocky, but they are important tools to help you move forward professionally and make a difference.

People Have a Place in Their Hearts for YPs

My twenties have taught me that people generally have a place in their hearts for young people who want to step up and be leaders. Some groups or individuals might be more outward and obvious about this while others might wait for a young professional to display positive characteristics before trusting them. As you continue on your journey in making a difference, you will experience people who do not believe that young people can lead well. However, these will pale in comparison to the larger set of people who will empower you to step up and serve in roles or help groups in specific ways.

Often times more seasoned professionals embrace young people. The sense of nostalgia seems to permeate within people when they are working in tandem with a young professional. They will talk about what it was like or how things operated in the business world when they were in their twenties or thirties. Simply, I think it makes them feel youthful again. Young professionals also bring an eagerness and energy that is appealing to seasoned workers. This type of partnership and relationship truly benefits both sides.

People also generally enjoy mentoring and love the idea of having a protégé that they can introduce to their friends and colleagues. By providing a young professional with opportunities, connections and experience, they feel as though they are laying out a formula for success to someone who they think can be great someday soon. Do not shy away from people who might be the same age as your parents, aunts, uncles or even grandparents. If you treat them with respect and ask for their support, they will start to see your successes as theirs.

Making the Golden Years More Enjoyable

As a kid I was always a little awkward around people who were in their 60s, 70s and beyond. I think that, like a lot of youngsters, I simply did not know, or at least thought I did not know, what to talk about with older folks. After having some good volunteering experiences with senior citizens during high school, I really embraced a nice annual event with my fraternity during

Thoughts for Leaders:

"You gain strength, courage and confidence by every experience in which you really stop to look fear in the face."

Eleanor Roosevelt

college. Each year the brothers of my fraternity had a Valentine's Day mixer at the local senior center. We played bingo, ate some healthy snacks, and enjoyed terrific conversations with the seniors. This was always my favorite community service oriented event because I really felt like we were making Valentine's Day weekend a lot more enjoyable for local seniors.

There are a number of ways in which you can help seniors. The most effective way is to call a local senior center and ask if they are accepting volunteers or about ways in which you can assist them. Another great way is to get involved in organizations that aid seniors. I have been on the board of directors of LifeSpan, Inc. since 2005 and have found it to be a rewarding opportunity. The mission of LifeSpan is to "provide life transition management through education, support and advocacy that identifies options, fosters self-respect, and is based on community and individual priorities." We manage a number of senior centers and also apartments for seniors and constantly try to find ways to provide increased opportunities for seniors. LifeSpan is just one example of a non-profit group that works with older adults. If you are interested in aiding older adults, I would encourage you to examine local groups where you could make a difference.

Ironically, as I was writing this section I actually had an amazing opportunity this afternoon to chaperone a group of the teens from the organization that I work for on a visit to the local senior center. Our teens created Halloween crafts and got to share them today with the seniors during the visit. I was touched to see how much our teens were able to brighten their day. I was also impressed with our host, Liz Catullo, who is a recent high school graduate and now works at the senior center while she is in college. She was incredibly kind to the seniors and I was happy to learn that her position there was a direct result of the volunteer work that she did there during her high school years. This visit reminded me that whether it is big or small, we can all make a difference in the lives of people in our community.

Different Than You

Do not be afraid to join a group in which you might be the minority. In college, I loved attending events organized by the Black Student Union and have always tried to attend events that were sponsored by all types of different people in Pittsburgh. Taking yourself out of your comfort zone is a good way to grow as a person and challenge yourself. It is extremely easy and natural to want to spend the majority of your time with the same people. Erin and I are no different and have a core group of friends that we play sports with, have game and poker nights with, and eat out with regularly. Spending quality time with the same group of people is not a problem, but it is important to attempt to branch out and meet new people. If you typically spend your time with people who are similar to you, the need to expand your social network is that much more important.

A club, board or committee that consists of 10-15 people who look alike, talk alike and act alike does very little to move its agenda forward. A mix of all types of people from diverse backgrounds is needed to freshen up programs, events and initiatives and enables groups to avoid becoming stagnant. As you examine opportunities that exist for growth and involvement in your community, I would recommend that you consider and participate in events and initiatives that are coordinated by people who are different than you.

A special story about my dad came from his time teaching at a school with a large African American enrollment in Pittsburgh. My father and his students got along incredibly well and had a great relationship. It always amazed me how natural my dad was in any type of group and I am sure this was no different. Caucasian professionals were not people that his students were accustomed to being close with, but my dad was very much the exception in this regard. When my dad brought a picture to school of my mom and him, the kids responded by saying, "Mr. Baker, what are you doing with that white woman?" The students had become so close to him that race didn't matter to anyone. I have always loved that story and feel that it illustrates the fact that we can and need to embrace and celebrate the similarities and differences that are present in all of us. There are enough hardships in life and the last thing we need to do is make enemies or remain apathetic toward one another because we might not look or talk like each other.

Pick up The Phone

We all generally learn something new about technology just about every day. In any given day I email, fax, instant message and text message with my professional colleagues. On many days I even talk to people who I work with on Facebook and MySpace. It is almost too easy

Thoughts for Leaders:

"The art of communication is the language of leadership."

James Humes

to get a message or note to someone without actually speaking with them. I think that we do a disservice to one another by always utilizing these other mechanisms to share information. There are many reasons why picking up the phone and giving someone a call can be beneficial to us all.

Since it is so easy to communicate in other ways, I usually correlate in my mind the fact that items discussed on phone calls are important. If someone gives me a call about work issues or items being discussed on boards and committees, I take even more notice about what they call to discuss. Talking on the phone also enables both parties to avoid the confusion and misinterpretations that often occur when business is done in emails.

As you work on projects and meet people with whom you would like to share a professional bond, I would recommend that you not shy away from calling them. If you are working on something specific, give them a call and get their feedback. Calling someone shows some guts and might even entice mentors to see you in a more professional light.

Third Life Crisis

I have heard the phrase, "Mid-Life Crisis" mentioned about people in their 40s and sometimes hear the idea of a quarter life crisis mentioned for 20-somethings. Even recording artist John Mayer mentioned this concept on his Room for Squares album. It might sound a little bit morbid, but I believe that we can go through a "Third Life Crisis" in our 20s and 30s. Because my dad passed away when he was young, I have always been aggressive and constantly set goals to accomplish things at a fairly young age. This can lead to me getting extremely frustrated and disappointed with myself from time to time. I mention to others that I have "Bill Clinton Syndrome" in this way. President Clinton's father passed away when he was extremely young, and in reading a great deal about his life, this sense of mortality seems to have been a big part of what caused Clinton to set high goals for himself that he expected to achieve at a young age.

If you are ambitious, your 20s and 30s can include rough patches. Since we are generally not our own bosses yet and have to appeal to others to get projects moving forward, it is possible to get frustrated about our professional status. It can even make us feel powerless and under whelmed. As we climb the ladders of our professional lives, we should all remember to empower our younger staff members and make them feel valued.

To avoid or effectively manage the "Third Life Crisis" I would remind you that feeling a bit unsatisfied with your professional development is common and that you are not odd for having these thoughts. Even people who I consider to be the most successful professionals locally in their 20s and 30s complain and feel badly about their shortcomings from time to time. As you move forward, stay positive and focus on how you can advance your career and make a difference as a leader in the areas that you care about.

Give a Fair Share of the Credit

As a leader, you will want to have those people who work with or for you enjoying following your guidance. You need to try your hardest to make them feel like a valuable part of your organization or group. It is vital to provide positive feedback to the people who participate and give of their time and talents to make your initiatives a success. When things are going well, make sure to share more than a fair share of the credit that you receive with them. When giving quotes to media sources or sending out messages, make sure to thank those working around you and speak as "we" instead of "I". It is a terrible feeling to be active with a group and see your chair or president taking all of the credit for what has been achieved or accomplished.

I have had three experiences in specifically adding recognition programs over the course of the last decade. As student body president at Millersville University I developed the Student Senator of the Year Award to honor a member who had worked tirelessly for the organization. Ironically, my wife ended up winning this award three years later for all that she did at our alma mater. As the director of Learning Ladder Child Development Center in Lancaster, I implemented a Student of the Week and Teacher of the Month recognition system. At the end of every month, I held a special breakfast for all of the students who were named Student of the Week and also acknowledged the Teacher of the Month. I was amazed to see how seriously both the students and staff took these honors and I loved being able to recognize how valuable they were to the school. Finally, as president of the Associates for Student

Thoughts for Leaders:

"Kind words can be short and easy to speak, but their echoes are truly endless."

Mother Theresa

Development (ASD) in my graduate school years at Indiana University of Pennsylvania, I implemented an award for the ASD Member of the Month. People generally do things for the right reasons, but I think it is extremely important to celebrate them both privately and also in a public manner for all of the good that they do.

I have often said that people want to be inspired, but too often have leaders who focus on negative things and motivate others to do

112

very little to move a group forward. By sharing the credit with those around you, everyone will win and you will enjoy more successes as a leader and hopefully either be asked back to your position or be at the forefront of others' minds for bigger challenges and more significant leadership opportunities.

If You Need Help, You Have To Ask

Some of the greatest business and political careers have started with a person who was able to simply convince their friends and family that they had an idea that could be either successful or profitable. This seems like an easy task, but too often the people in our inner circle are the ones who squash our hopes and dreams by bringing us back down when we are thinking big. Your loved ones generally want you to succeed, but too often worry about the chance that you will fail, in large part because they care about you. To gather the support of your family and friends, I would encourage you to show your true passion for your idea or concept and also provide them with a framework of how you are going to accomplish your goals. Do not be afraid to get a little pumped up when you talk to them about your idea, but also make sure to stay grounded a bit in reality. You want them to be convinced that you have a big dream that is possible to be achieved. From my own experience and through leaders that I have studied, it has become clear that so many people who were able to achieve in a big way do so with very little initial support beyond their family and friends.

Once you get your family and friends on board and they believe in your concept, it is vital to keep them busy and provide them with specific tasks. The same holds true as your network continues to grow and expand. Volunteers and supporters want to be given various ways in which they can make a positive impact in what you are doing. They also want to feel as though they are part of a winning team that is making a difference. Remind them regularly of the progress that you all are making and thank them for their service and commitment to helping you realize your dreams.

Since the financial piece is generally so crucial in starting a business, organizing a new club or planning an event, it is important to think creatively about ways to bring in funds. The same strategies that you utilize to get your family and friends involved can be implemented when talking to potential funders. Wealthy citizens, corporations and foundations all want to be part of successful ventures and will look for positive qualities in you that compliment the good Ideas that you have. Money will certainly not be thrown at you. I have seen a lot of good business ideas, community groups and candidates get stalled because they are unable to raise money. Too often we rely on the fact that people will proactively finance the initiatives that make us passionate. While this happens on rare occasions, it is essential to ask constantly for ideas, volunteers and financial donations if you want to move forward in making your dreams come true.

Don't Be Scared of Powerful People

If you want to make a difference, you will need to garner the support of the power players who have influence and access to resources. There are a number of techniques that you can use to help make these leaders part of your extended or even inner network. While it is very important to be professional and polite, it is also vital that you be aggressive in seeking out ways to get your message across to these stakeholders. When you see power players at events or meetings, do not shy away from introducing yourself to them and tell them a little bit about the project or initiative that you would like them to support. If you have met them before and they do not seem to recognize you, it is completely appropriate to re-introduce yourself. I think we all end up eating some "humble pie" in these situations from time to time. Try and make sure that your business card makes its way into either their pocket or into the hands of their aide or assistant. Having a cordial relationship with the people who work for them is a good way to have your doors opened. While the power player might be intimidating, it will be much easier to acquire access and interest from the people who work in their company or organization.

It is also vital to have a clear sense of what you want from someone before talking with them. I have seen people who get in front of the person who could help them in their ventures, but they either freeze up around them or have not prepared what they would say in such a situation. Have a script prepared in your mind of

Thoughts for Leaders:

"Keep your fears to yourself, but share your courage with others."

Robert Lewis Stevenson

what you will say if you get 90 seconds to chat with a power broker at an event this week. You are better off coming across as too organized than being seen as unsure of yourself and what you want to accomplish. The most basic items that you could mention to them are financial items (donation or sponsorship) or their physical support (attending an event, being on a host committee or giving a keynote address). Be direct, but also remain a bit fluid with what you hope to accomplish out of the relationship. It is far better to get them on your side in a lesser role now than to ostracize them if they offer a commitment that was not part of your original plan. The truth is that you will most likely need their financial or physical support in the future. Besides the good feeling or rush that comes from these conversations, they also will enable you to raise more money or develop better events. And, like all things, you will get better at making the most of your opportunities to speak with powerful people as you get more experience doing it.

You Only Get What You Give

It is very likely that you have heard a friend or colleague at one point blame an organization for not providing them with opportunities. It is true that paid staff members and board or committee leaders certainly need to do their part in organizing effectively and planning strategically to involve members in the core mission of any group. However, the responsibility for getting involved in a group falls on the shoulders of only one person – YOU!

In the late 1990s a band named The New Radicals had a hit song called, "You Only Get What You Give". I think this song title holds so true when considering our personal involvements with our groups. If you expect someone to come and hold your hand to get involved, it most likely will not happen and you will be disappointed. However, if you are willing to step out of your comfort zone and ask leaders in the organization to aid you in getting involved, you are much more likely to have a positive experience.

Joining organizations simply to improve or lengthen your resume is a terrible reason to pay dues. If you are not prepared or willing to get involved and become a "do-er" within an organization, you are better off spending your money elsewhere. As you examine the groups with which you are currently involved, think about specific ways that you are giving back right now. If you can't come up with much as you are analyzing your commitments, I would encourage you to develop a plan for how you can become more of a leader within your organization. This type of brainstorming will also be effective when you are thinking about joining new groups, organizations or committees.

When you are giving of yourself to a cause that you care about and are committed to, it will not seem like it is work or a nagging obligation. The rewards from giving back to things that you care about are truly priceless. Please remember that no one else but you is to blame it you feel like a group is letting you down as a member. By putting the responsibility on yourself, you will take much more ownership of both the success of the group and your personal growth as a valuable member.

Be the Hungriest Person You Know

In September 2007, PUMP was one of the host organizations for the PA ImPAct Conference. This conference was a great way for young professionals to network with one another and to learn best practices initiatives that other groups were working on and planning in their cities and communities.

There was a great panel that included a young business leader named Luke Skurman. Skurman started a company called College Prowler which provides guides to students on hundreds of college campuses and has reached one million

Thoughts for Leaders:

"Only those who dare to fail greatly can ever achieve greatly."

Robert F. Kennedy

dollars a year of sales annually. I cannot express how impressed I was with Skurman and what he has achieved in the five years since he began his business at the age of 22. Skurman was part of a panel with three other young business owners who all seemed very proud and content with the progress of their companies. They were doing well and should have been proud. What really struck me most were Skurman's answers. He was by far the most successful person on the panel from a revenue and growth perspective, but was the only one who said he was never really happy with how much he had achieved to this point. He was proud, but admitted that he is never really satisfied. I think this is a pretty good mentality for us all to adopt and embrace.

We should certainly feel a sense of pride in what we do. Still, it seems that the people who are never really satisfied will build big businesses or achieve amazing things at a young age. I want to encourage you to always be hungry for the next big thing. If we rest too much on what we have achieved in the past, it will become very easy to become stagnant and not grow as a leader. If you have not tried anything new or undertaken a challenging project in the last six months, I suggest you take a look around and see what else you could be doing. It takes a sense of hunger and passion to make a difference and I would encourage you to tackle new challenges regularly. Also, try and maintain professional and personal relationships with people who you think seem hungry and anxious to continue achieving and improving themselves. These people will keep you feeling motivated and are also terrific advisors from whom to solicit advice and feedback. When we stop taking advantage of enrichment opportunities, we very quickly can stop growing and developing as agents of positive change.

Two for the Price of One

President Bill Clinton made the saying "two for the price of one" pretty famous during his presidential campaign in 1992. When on the campaign trail, Clinton would often mention that if you elected him you would also receive the expertise, ideas and leadership capabilities of his spouse, Hillary Rodham Clinton. The core sentiment within this message is something that I think is important to consider when we are dating and considering a spouse. Finding someone as a partner for life who motivates you and who also wants to make a difference is really important. It can be quite telling to talk to spouses or significant others of your colleagues because you can learn a lot about what drives or motivates the person with whom you work.

My wife and I share a number of the same passions and both work a great deal to help attract and retain young professionals in the greater Pittsburgh region. Sharing interests is great because you can go to events together, sit on similar committees and occasionally even plan events in tandem. I really enjoyed serving as co-chairs of Discover Pittsburgh together in 2006 and was so proud that I could rely on my spouse to be such an effective and efficient partner in planning and executing our plan. I am an active person and have a new idea or goal daily. My wife is great at challenging me to work toward achieving my dreams. She also doesn't shy away from expressing to me when she thinks that opportunities are not a solid fit for me.

If you are already married or in a long-term relationship, I would encourage you to keep an interest in what your "better half" is doing in their professional life and through extracurricular activities. Support them, provide them with ideas and encourage them to achieve their goals.

If you are single, I would simply suggest that you consider what type of partner will keep you focused and inspire you to be a passionate and productive person. These things might not be quite as obvious as other factors when you begin dating someone, but they will influence you indefinitely either in a negative or positive manner. Your partner can be your biggest fan and supporter or someone who holds you back from the amazing things you want to do. Think about growing your relationship or finding a relationship that demonstrates the best possibilities in what Clinton referenced when he suggested the concept of getting "two for the price of one".

Quantify Everything

When I started working at Carnegie Mellon, I was taken aback by how much I heard the term "quantify" used. The students there were incredibly intelligent and had amazing skill sets and understood how important it is to quantify your goals, your progress and hopefully, your achievements. We live in a world that loves numbers. As a sports fan I can proudly admit to you that I generally know the batting averages of baseball players, the number of touchdown passes a quarterback throws and the points a basketball player averages per game. The same holds true in politics, which is a competitive beast that breeds a focus on numbers.

When you are managing events, programs or committees, I would strongly suggest that you set specific goals for how much money you want to raise, how many people you hope to reach or any other relevant statistic that would make your work deemed successful. You will want to get your team on board with these goals and make sure that they are committed to the goals that have been established. Get them involved in the process so they feel personally committed to the process.

As a fan of numbers, I always make sure to keep a good count on how many people attend events that I plan or help manage. It is also important to keep good records and be able to showcase how much has been raised through an initiative. In talking with power players, you will want to be able to talk in specifics as opposed to speaking in generalities. People will not want to know how an event made you feel, but will want to know specifics about how it affected your community or organization.

While we are on the subject of communicating in terms that are quantifiable and not based solely on opinion or feeling, I would like to make a quick pitch regarding your resume and cover letter. Take a look at your resume soon and

Thoughts for Leaders:

"The will to win is important, but the will to prepare is vital."

Joe Paterno

check to see if you use many specific numbers on it. Employers like to see details in your resume of what you have done in a way that lacks feeling. When working with students in the past, I have always encouraged them to start each bullet with a different action verb. After the action verb, I would suggest that you consider including specific numbers regarding what you have accomplished in your previous professional work, in your community efforts or during your educational experiences. Moving forward, it is important to think about communicating in terms that are more quantifiable. Make sure to continue to showcase the great things that you are doing with a focus on numbers and statistics.

Be Yourself

It is always a little concerning to witness friends and colleagues who change drastically when they embark upon a new stage in their lives. If you have been successful and had an easy time making friends and gaining respect in the past, I would suggest that you not make any significant shift in the way that you present yourself or communicate within groups. Changing the way that you behave or letting go of something that people associate with you can confuse others and make them feel less close to you.

If you have enjoyed planning meetings and events during your previous experience, make sure that you keep doing this as you progress. In a similar manner, it is also vital to not completely adapt your personality or communication style based on those who are surrounding you. Of course, you will need to dress or speak in a different manner at a business meeting than you do at dinner with your friends. However, I would just suggest that you not try to overcompensate in new situations. Doing this can unfortunately make you come across as fake or uncomfortable in your own skin. Being yourself in all that you do will allow others to really connect with you and give an impression that reflects the real type of person that you are.

I have had what sometimes comes across as an unprofessional nickname since I was less than a week old. When I was a newborn I received the nickname "Chugger" because I was such a thirsty baby and chugged away at endless amounts of milk in the nursery. My parents and family stuck with the name and when I got to school it became what my teachers called me. I can honestly say that in my 19 years of being a student I had less than five teachers/professors, administrators and coaches call me anything but Chugger. It simply was my identity and I think represents my fun-natured and enthusiastic mentality. When I started running for School Board in 2005 I really began to hide away from the name that had been a big part of my life for the previous 25 years. Wow, what a mistake. As I shied away from the name, I could actually feel myself becoming less friendly, less energetic, stiff and overly serious when I was talking with other people. As I continue to quickly approach my thirties, I have decided to embrace the name that has been a big part of me for my entire life again. If we talk in the future, please feel free to call me Tom or Chugger. I now ask people to call me whatever they feel most comfortable with and find that most people opt for the milk-oriented name.

If there is something that has played a big role in your life, I would ask that you make an effort to keep it with you as you continue on your professional journey. This unique characteristic or trait might be something as simple as a nickname that you have or a hobby that you enjoy. I know a lot of people in their twenties and thirties who have some really creative and even sometimes quirky interests outside of work. Embrace what makes you a little different than your friends and colleagues and proudly share it with them. Who knows, you might help others become more honest and open about things that make them tick.

Spam Your Friends

One of my favorite characters on television is the role that Steve Carell plays as Michael Scott on "The Office". If you haven't watched the show, I would highly recommend it because it is extremely funny. It will teach you some interesting lessons about good and bad strategies in motivating and inspiring others. One of Scott's unprofessional behaviors on the show is his enjoyment in forwarding inappropriate email messages to his staff. While what Michael Scott does certainly is not a good habit to undertake, sending along quality and important messages to your friends and colleagues can be useful and helpful. I always really appreciate it when people I know send along notices and invitations regarding fundraisers and community events. This is a good way to help raise awareness and funds for causes that you care about for no cost.

People within your network want to know more about what is going on in the community. Even if they do not respond or help with regard to the information you distribute, they will benefit from your efforts. It also sometimes takes multiple points of contact before someone decides to get involved or support a charity or community effort. Your message can simply be a part of this public relations effort on behalf of something you care about. We all cannot be everywhere and know everything that is taking place in our community, so it is vital that we keep each other posted on upcoming events.

When sending along the information to your colleagues, I would recommend that you keep it simple. Make sure you include the date, time, location, cost and ways that people can sponsor or support the cause. If RSVPs are needed in a

Thoughts for Leaders:

"My best friend is the one that brings out the best in me."

Henry Ford

timely manner, make sure to point out deadlines and a contact person in your message. I also find it much more appealing to support something a friend is passionate about when they showcase their thoughts and feelings in the message. Make sure to tell people why what you are sending them is important to you and how it will make a difference in the community or world. Dropping a few names of people who have already committed to attending an event or supporting a charity will also make people feel more inclined to get involved.

As you continue receiving messages from people you know, I would encourage you to take a serious look at the information that you have been sent. If something is important to your friends, then you owe it to them to sincerely review their information. By supporting each other in a reciprocal fashion you can multiply the impact that you and the people within your network are making.

Traveling In A Way That Works For You

Admittedly, I am not the poster child for being a good world traveler. I am not a fan of planes and can get pretty restless on trips. I am becoming a bit of a better traveler as I get older and was happy to feel very relaxed and at ease on the cruise to the Bahamas that I took with my wife and friends last summer. Despite my minor complaints and impatience, I have enjoyed some really enriching traveling experiences during my twenties as well. We all generally get busier, more responsibility and more tied down to where we live everyday. This isn't a bad thing and generally means that we are growing and becoming more influential in our leadership journey. No matter how hectic your schedule gets, it is vital to plan some time away from home. It can be a nice big vacation or a series of weekend trips. The specific plan isn't as important as it is to simply have one. We can love our city or town a great deal and will need to get away from time to time. There is a certain refreshing feeling that comes from leaving town for a few days to experience a new location.

Many of the friends that you have made thus far in your life most likely live across your state and around the country. Some others might even be living abroad. Visiting friends where they live is a great way to travel and will enable you to cut costs on your trip by having free lodging. You can also get a free built-in tour guide by staying with a friend. Erin and I love traveling to visit our friends and it is always great to experience a new town or community. You can check out local diners, museums, sporting venues and so many other must-see tourist attractions and locations. When people express interest in staying with you, it is important to showcase the town where you live and demonstrate what makes your community special and unique. When friends visit us in Pittsburgh, we love taking them to the Heinz History Center, to a baseball game a PNC Park, to see the incline and to a few of the great restaurants that our city features.

I encourage you to find a few weekends in the next six months in which you could afford to get away and plan trips to visit friends from high school, college or graduate school or even former co-workers from past jobs. Also, lock down a couple of weekends in which friends that you haven't seen in awhile could come out and stay with you. You won't regret it and, who knows, you might even attract or recruit a good friend to move to your city.

There Goes My Hero

I have always really enjoyed learning about people, particularly famous leaders and personalities who have influenced our country. There is something fascinating about studying the people who intrigue you and in some way motivate you to become a better person. Having heroes that we know is definitely important. Family members or mentors who are in your life and that you look up to are essential and I do not want to take away from these special bonds in any way. I do want to ask you to think about a few of the leaders or historic figures that really make you curious or have motivated you in the past. Take a minute or two and jot down their names.

Who are your heroes?

_____

_____

_____

_____

_____

Then I would like for you to consider the following questions:

1.) How did they get to where they are?

2.) What makes them tick?

3.) What have they overcome in their lives?

4.) What are the most important skills or talents that they possess?

You might be able to answer these questions easily or you could be unsure of some of the answers. Either way, I would suggest trying a Google search and locating a book about this person. Biographies and autobiographies are a terrific way to get inside the heads of the people we admire. You will learn about the answers to the four questions that I mentioned above and so much more.

The people who I have studied and learned about over the years include Ronald Reagan, Donald Trump, Martin Luther King, Jr., Abraham Lincoln and Rudy Giuliani. I have always enjoyed reading about business executives and governmental leaders who are currently doing big things or have accomplished large feats. Learning about public officials who have led in times of national or local crisis has also always intrigued me. In any given month I probably read at least one or two books about people who I think have made a positive impact on our society.

One great thing that we can take from reading about our heroes is that they are not perfect and, for the most part, have had to overcome obstacles and hardships in their professional and personal lives. It will make you feel better about yourself and enable you to believe that you can achieve the type of success that your heroes have. Our heroes seem so powerful and successful to us now. Still, reading about their upbringing and what they did during their 20s and 30s really humanizes who they are and how they ascended into power. By studying our heroes we can learn how to lead more effectively and become better agents of change in our communities. Pick up a book about one of your heroes today!

Admit When You're Wrong

One of my favorite quotes has always been that "a good leader takes more than their fair share of the blame and gives more than their share of the credit." We all love working with visionary leaders who make us feel part of the team, who demonstrate a sincere passion for what is being done and who help move groups to new levels of excellence. These leaders are a direct contrast from those who make it seem like they did everything by themselves, who toss blame around to colleagues when things do not go well and do not truly seem to care about the mission or goals of the organization.

The first type of leader makes us try harder than we ever expected we could while the other makes us want to call off work or drop out of a committee or board. Think about these short descriptions and consider someone who fits into each group of leader. What do you enjoy or dislike about working with each of them? How have they motivated you or stifled your performance? Study both of these people and spend time comparing yourself to each. Are there things that you do that might make others feel uninspired or negative when you are leading?

How can you become more like the person who you noted as a great motivator in your life? Since none of us are perfect, it is inevitable that we will make mistakes from time to time. How we handle these mistakes will tell a lot to others about what type of leader and person we are.

When I am underachieving or not doing well in my commitments I will often tell people the exact reason why I am coming up short. I think people appreciate when you are sincere and are more inclined to forgive or understand your shortcomings. We all have times when things get extremely busy, family issues arise or we simply drop the ball on a project. Don't make excuses. Simply apologize and explain what happened. By getting the facts out there you will not enable people to start rumors or guess why you have not been on top of your game. As soon as you apologize and explain your actions, immediately work tirelessly to improve the situation by getting the work done.

We have all seen mistakes that turn into bigger deals than they needed to be. Ineffective leaders seem to have a way of turning minor situations into front-page newspaper catastrophes. Keep the facts out there and do not hide from what has happened in these situations. In these times of what feels like a crisis, you will need to bring people together and not divide the group. Admitting your shortcomings will show the humility that resides within you.

When I was 23 and director of one of The Learning Ladder schools in Lancaster, I had to deal with a really tough situation. One of the kids in our Tiny Tots classrooms (ages 1-2) fell and cracked his head open and was bleeding profusely. As I am writing this, I can still picture Dylan's face as he was brought into my office. I don't think I had ever been so scared in my life. I immediately got his mom on the phone and he was with her en-route to the hospital five minutes later. His mom and aunt yelled at me relentlessly. I didn't try to be defensive or yell back. I just told them that I would do whatever it took to make sure this never happened again and that I was so sorry that it happened to Dylan. After getting stitched up, Dylan came back to school a few days later. I really made a point to communicate with his family and ask them about how it went and what I could do. Dylan ended up being one of my favorite kids in the school. He would often yell out "Tom" and loved hanging in my office. We even ended up wearing matching white dress shirts, khaki pants and navy ties on "Twin Day" at the school. His family could have sued us, could have pulled him out of the school or even just spread negative things about our center to others. Instead, they became great ambassadors for us and were happy customers. Handling touch situations is never a fun task, but the way you react to them will show others a great deal about what type of leader you are.

Inspiring Volunteerism

Participating in community service has always been something that I have enjoyed. My parents were both very active in our community so I was brought up assuming that volunteering was something that most people did. Unfortunately, this assumption was incorrect. We need more people to get involved in community service in an effort to make our communities stronger and improve the lives of our neighbors. Community service needs to be a part, even it it is minor, of everyone's life. I wanted to share with you about Pittsburgh Cares and encourage you to learn about what groups are providing similar services in your city or town. I have had the honor to serve on the board of directors of Pittsburgh Cares for the last two years and am continually astounded by the amazing number of local citizens who participate in service projects. We also have an amazing executive director, Daniel Horgan, and a great staff that works extremely hard to build new partnerships and provide enriching experiences for volunteers of all ages.

The mission of Pittsburgh Cares is to "inspire volunteerism by organizing flexible and rewarding service projects that impact critical needs in greater Pittsburgh." I think the story of Pittsburgh Cares is amazing and I wanted to share it with you. "In August 1992, six Pittsburgh friends joined together to found Pittsburgh Cares. They wanted to offer local volunteer opportunities, especially for those who found it difficult to volunteer often or on a regular schedule. Pittsburgh Cares was one of the first affiliates in what is now Hands on Network (formerly CityCares), with affiliates across the USA and overseas. Using the flexible, episodic volunteering model, Pittsburgh Cares began offering its volunteers a monthly calendar of community service opportunities to choose from. Since then, Pittsburgh Cares has grown

Thoughts for Leaders:

"A leader's role is to raise people's aspirations for what they can become and to release their energies so they will try to get there."

David Gergen

tremendously and now has a base of 3,000 volunteers in Pittsburgh, a downtown office with a professional staff, a board of directors and an advisory board. We have formal relationships with some 100 service agencies for work each year to help them deliver their services. Pittsburgh Cares is a 501 (c) 3 tax-exempt organization and we rely on corporate, foundation, and individual contributions for our operating expenses. Over the years, Pittsburgh Cares has contributed hundreds of thousands of hours of volunteer support to non-profit organizations in greater Pittsburgh." (from www.pittsburghcares.org)

Find out if your city has an organization like Pittsburgh Cares that you can join or where you can learn about volunteering opportunities. If not, think about taking the plunge like the Pittsburgh Cares founders did in 1992 and start an organization or club that will organize community service opportunities and empower local residents to make a difference.

Volunteering is a great way to get your hands "dirty" in your community and can be a nice way to make new friends. No matter where you live, there are ways to get involved in community service. Get active at your local soup kitchen, senior center, little league or at your place of worship. There is no excuse for not volunteering at least modestly every year because of the limitless chances that exist to help others. I challenge you to sign up today to do something that will positively influence the lives of others!

Partying for a Purpose

The PGH Party for a Purpose is the perfect example of how an incredibly simple and basic concept can make a huge difference. The mission of PGH Party for a Purpose is to host "fun, creative, and affordable parties for diverse

> **Thoughts for Leaders:**
>
> *"It's easy to make a buck. It's a lot tougher to make a difference."*
>
> Tom Brokaw

young-minded individuals, while raising funds and generating support for nonprofit organizations in Southwestern Pennsylvania." The founding group consists of three young professionals, Julie Pezzino, Jessica Obergas, and Vivien Luk. All three of them have good jobs with some of the most reputable and respected organizations in the region. It is obvious that they did not organize PGH Party for a Purpose to make money for themselves, but instead to assist groups who are trying to help others.

These three women started raising funds for non-profits in the fall of 2006 and average close to $2,000 per party. They provide attendees with refreshments, entertainment, and a quality venue in which to mingle. The groups that are selected receive a good deal of positive exposure and also are able to raise significant funds while doing minimal work. Still a fairly new concept, Julie, Jessica, and Vivien manage a professional application process for potential beneficiaries and have caught the eye of many leaders in the non-profit sector. This model of raising funds is definitely one that could and should be adapted and organized in other cities. I am so impressed with what these three friends have done to showcase quality organizations and fundraise for them while enabling thousands of people a year to have a fun time on weekend evenings.

A colleague and regular participant of PGH Party for a Purpose, Regina Anderson, said, "If you think you're too busy to volunteer, this is a great way to introduce yourself to a philanthropic cause. It makes people believe that they can make a difference. This effort went from an ad-hoc group of friends to an organized business model that has a long waiting list of non-profits that want to get on board." This is a story that should inspire us all to think about ways we can help groups in our cities that provide such vital and necessary services with only shoe string budgets and limited resources.

The Networker of the Year

While I was working as Paul Snatchko's campaign manager in 2006, I had the pleasure of meeting Chaz Kellem. While Paul was doing some outreach at a Pittsburgh Colts (semi professional football team) game, we were trying to track down a guy named Chaz. I could tell almost immediately that he was a popular person. All of the interns and staff who were working with him just seemed to love him. I later came across him when we were going through a training program to become participants in a new type of initiative through electronic mentoring. Again, I was impressed with Chaz. Shortly thereafter he invited me to become part of the Community Bridge Building Network (CBBN). The CBBN meets monthly and is a terrific group helping connect business and civic leaders without requiring dues or any burdensome commitment. I was really happy that he asked me to be part of this great group.

What I haven't mentioned so far about Chaz is that he has a physical disability that requires him to spend almost all of his time in a wheelchair. He suffers from a disease called Osteogenesis Imperfecta, a disorder that allows bones to break easily and generally for no obvious reason. You may have heard it referred to as the "brittle bone" disorder. According to the Osteogenesis Imperfecta Foundation website (www.oif.org) people can break a rib while laughing or a leg while sleeping. In no way does Chaz let his disability tie him down or limit the impact that he makes on the region. His professional pursuits include his position as a Group Sales Account Executive for the Pittsburgh Pirates and the General Manager of the Pittsburgh Colts. Even more impressively, he sits on three non-profit boards and a number of committees. We often find ourselves thinking that this Chaz guy is everywhere!

On October 18, 2007 Chaz was in front of the room at a well-attended conference organized by the CBBN. He and some of his peers were nominated for the highest honor to be given out that day, the Networker of the Year. As his name was read as the winner I found myself a little choked up. I had never felt so happy or proud to see someone get an award. It amazes me to think about Chaz and how negative, bitter, or cynical he could be. While many of us find difficulty in such unimportant things that have little impact on our lives, Chaz continues to keep moving forward with an incredibly positive and upbeat spirit. At a recent panel he reminded the crowd that "every day is a blessing". It is so refreshing to hear from and know someone who has such a great outlook on life. What makes it even more inspiring is that it comes from someone who hasn't been presented with many luxuries and who has been through some really

Thoughts for Leaders:

"Show me someone who has done something worthwhile, and I'll show you someone who has overcome adversity."

Lou Holtz

tough and serious circumstances. Still, Chaz encourages us all to get out there and make a difference and focus on the positive things that are happening around us. We all need to be more like Chaz Kellem, Pittsburgh's Networker of the Year.

Teen Oasis is My Therapy

I am currently the executive director of a non-profit organization, Healthy Teens, Inc. We operate and manage a teen center in Monroeville, Teen Oasis. To date, Teen Oasis has over 300 members, averages 25-35 teens in attendance daily, and hosted over 100 events in 2007. It is a great organization which really makes an important difference in the lives of teens living in the eastern suburbs of Pittsburgh. While I would love to tell you about what is going on at Teen Oasis, I instead want to share with you the amazing story of how this group and teen center began. More importantly, I want to share with you about a small group of people who really set out to change a community.

Jeff Tobe, Bonnie Kridler, and Colleen Pietrusinki became friends while sitting on the board of the Gateway Foundation in Monroeville. During focus group meetings, the teens expressed that they needed a place to "hang out" and engage in healthy recreation. The local ice skating rink and movie theater both were shut down, greatly reducing the positive places for local teens to spend their time. Instead of ignoring these sentiments, Jeff, Bonnie, and Colleen, along with other leaders and concerned citizens, set out on a journey that has influenced a region. In the organizing weeks and months, they got their hands extremely dirty, both literally and metaphorically. They secured a location from the local hospital, painted the building, applied for grants, hired a staff, completed endless paperwork, opened bank accounts, and gave more time than they would ever be willing to admit. Even when they faced setbacks or rejection, they worked harder and harder. They would not stop until teens were able to experience a safe and secure center that would

Thoughts for Leaders:

"Happiness comes to those who are moving toward something they want very much to happen. And it almost always involves making someone else happy."

Earl Nightingale

be drug, alcohol, and tobacco free. It required them taking time away from their families and using more connections and resources than most of us would ever even consider tapping.

Their story is amazing and one that I think should motivate us all to think of what we can do to help the people living in our neighborhood or region. Teen Oasis opened its doors in October 2005 and hasn't stopped helping teens since. The level of commitment from these outstanding leaders also has not subsided and we are fortunate to have a dedicated and hard working board of directors. Jeff and Bonnie lead the organization as president and vice president, respectively. They are two of the most special people I have ever met and I feel fortunate to work with them every day.

Teen Oasis works with an incredibly diverse assortment of teens daily. I often tell people that I have never seen a place in which a group of people get along so well, despite there being such an overwhelming cross-section of race, religion, and socio-economic backgrounds. One member, a 7th grader named Cameron, even recently said, "Teen Oasis is my therapy." This touching quote was a nice reminder of what an incredible difference Jeff, Bonnie, and Colleen made by embracing the thoughts of local teens and not settling until their vision came to fruition. We can all learn from the story of Teen Oasis that a small group of people really can achieve great things by working together and utilizing every possible resource that they have accumulated.

They show us that if you are committed and relentless, just about anything is possible.

Marketing by Walking Around

The phrase "managing by walking around" has tended to be trendy in business over the last few decades. The concept suggests that you can influence others and lead more effectively by simply seeing how others are doing and through interacting with them. It actually makes some sense to me and I agree that it is important to be visible and let others know that you care about their work and the issues that they are experiencing. A concept that I want you to consider is the idea of marketing by walking around. I would like for you to think of yourself as a potential moving billboard for what you care and feel strongly about. What you wear and your willingness to promote causes, organizations, educational institutions, businesses, and people can give them a tremendous amount of positive exposure. We can help recruit members, students, customers, and clients for what we believe in by simply wearing shirts, hats, and other items that include the logos or symbolize the message behind subjects for which we have passion.

I have always been a big believer in the concept of promoting the things you care about by walking around. I learned this as the recruitment chairman of my fraternity in college and have never lost faith in this concept since. We spend so much time and effort designing catchy posters, websites, and other promotional pieces. Having a good marketing plan is important for any group, campaign or company and I don't want to take away from that. However, simply having people walking around with a t-shirt or hat can make such an impression on others and spark interest in dozens if not hundreds of people on any given day. As a society, we are definitely curious and generally find interest in what others are wearing. Instead of promoting clothing companies by sporting items that showcase their brand, why not help create some grassroots buzz

Thoughts for Leaders:

"Trends, like horses, are easier to ride in the direction they are going."

John Naisbitt

for a non-profit group, business, political candidate, or school that you feel passionately about?

I would encourage you to think about the types of things that you could promote. As executive director of a non-profit I definitely try to help promote Teen Oasis, the teen center that we manage in the eastern suburbs of Pittsburgh. I regularly wear Teen Oasis sweatshirts and t-shirts and also try to make sure that our Teen Oasis pens get into as many hands as possible. Erin and I also wear an arsenal of attire from Millersville University, where we did our undergraduate work. It is my hope that middle school or high school students might see us and get curious about our college. Teen Oasis and Millersville are not the only two ways that I promote by walking around. I try to get some exposure for other non-profits, candidates, and organizations. What are three groups that you could help by spreading their message in this fashion? If you do not have a piece of clothing that has their logo or message, either buy one or ask for an extra item from them soon.

Please make sure to take a look around and see what other people are promoting. If we expect others to support us, we have to play a reciprocal role. I often times will notice someone wearing something new or different when I am out and will do an internet search about a cause or group later that day. Also, if you are in a social situation, it can be useful to ask questions to someone about what their clothing item is all about. You never know what positive movement or group you might learn about or even become a part of. Marketing by walking around is definitely what you make out of it. While you might never know the big impact it makes in the lives of others or the groups that you are promoting, it will make a difference.

How a Few People Enabled Thousands to Play Sports

I wanted to share with you an article that I originally wrote for the Pittsburgh Sports League (PSL) quarterly newsletter, "Sports Shorts", in the summer of 2005. It was to acknowledge the five year anniversary of the existence of the sports league and showcases the story of how the league began. Today, PSL has over 10,000 participants annually and has continued to organize both trusted fan favorites and new competitions for participants. Year round people of all ages can be found engaging in athletic competition throughout Western PA playing sports including flag football, deck hockey, bowling, basketball, softball, darts, broomball, soccer, and even the new popular game - corn hole. This has become a movement that helps thousands of people get active, lose weight, exercise regularly, make friends, and feel more connected to their community. Here is the story of how it all got started.

Five years ago the Pittsburgh Sports League became an important staple in the Pittsburgh region and a consistently growing facet of PUMP. What started as a dream for PSL founders Drew Elste, Daniel Casciato, Sara Salmon-Cox and

Michelle Blacksberg, became a reality after securing the support of PUMP in 2000. The four founders met through a softball league in Lawrenceville and according to Sara, it became evident quickly that there was an unmet demand for an all-around sports league. "We wanted to create a one-stop shop for adult co-ed sports," said Daniel. "In creating the league, we also felt that this would become another social outlet for young people in the region." The first PSL sport offered was flag football, which debuted in the fall of 2000. Bowling and volleyball were added for the winter season and

Thoughts for Leaders:

"Jump into the middle of things, get your hands dirty, fall flat on your face, and then reach for the stars."

Joan L. Curcio

by spring 2001, deck hockey, basketball, darts, billiards and volleyball were part of PSL's repertoire. Drew, Daniel, Sara and Michelle saw a great deal of potential for PSL to grow exponentially and also provide a sense of community with Pittsburgh. "Participating on a sports team gives you the opportunity to make stronger connections and form lasting friendships," said Michelle. "The PSL makes it easier for young professionals to grow roots here and therefore harder to move away." Sara feels that PSL thrives because of "the sense of community." She also noted that PSL can be "therapeutic" and can be a good break from work on even the most difficult days. The PSL is the premier provider of adult recreational sports leagues and in the last five years, over 5,000 Pittsburghers have been part of 400 teams in 75 different leagues. The PSL has received attention from the local media and was featured on National Public Radio's Morning Edition in the fall of 2003.

While PSL often comes across as a fine-tuned machine today, the original leagues required a great deal of work from the founders. Sara said that in the beginning they were involved in making schedules, ordering shirts, securing fields and referees. Those in charge also had to create rules for all of the sports and recruit players to participate in the newly formed league. Michelle estimates that they spent between 20-30 hours a week ensuring that the league would function in a professional manner. The leadership group expanded within a few months of its founding. Kristy Grecni and Peter Ten Hagen became vital to the growth of PSL. PUMP also agreed to fund a paid position solely designated to orchestrating the sports league.

Becky Reitmeyer, who currently serves as Director of PSL, said the PSL creates an environment for making friends because you see the same faces week after week, season after season. Beyond the preparation and sweat equity that it has taken to make PSL successful, the support from the local community and PSL participants has been vital. "I would like to personally thank all the PSL players who have told their friends about the fun and continue to play each season-the PSL would not be the same without your support," said Michelle. "PSL participants are very giving," added Becky. "They want to play; they want the league to grow and succeed. They give feedback, adjust their schedules to make games happen, help acquire facilities. Players don't just take part in the games, they participate in every aspect of the league." Daniel agreed. "They're the ones who make it successful. Without them, we would have had to pack our bags and go home."

The potential for PSL to continue growing appears to be quite possible. As new sports, including dodge ball, spark more interest in the league, partnerships are also being built with other groups. PSL and Girls Hope recently joined forces for Kickball for Hope, which is now an annual joint fundraiser. "We ventured into the partnership with the intention of making the tournament bigger and better than previous years and we've succeeded," said Becky.

As far as the future goes, Daniel hopes to see the PSL double in size and eventually build its own recreational facility, which was one of the goals of the original founders. Michelle also envisions the base of participation growing to more than double the current level and also sees tremendous potential for increased sponsorship in the years to come. Although the original founders are no longer involved in the management and direction of the league, their simple idea for Pittsburghers to have a place to play has made a tremendous impact on the lives of many young people in the region.

The PSL is an amazing model that could be modeled in other cities and regions. If you are interested in starting a league in your community I would encourage you to visit www.pump.org or www.pittsburghsportsleague.net. It also show-cases the fact that a small group of people can get thousands of people active and involved by having a dream and working hard to see it come true.

Be an Active "Friend" Raiser

If you hope to achieve great things in your career and through service opportunities, it is going to be imperative to have people who you can ask for support. When meeting someone, you never know what impact this person may have in your life both today and in the future. I have always been a bit of a "people collector" and don't like to lose track of the terrific individuals that I have met through my professional, educational, and civic experiences. We truly only are as good as the people who we have behind and beside us and building connections and bridges continually is important in achieving your goals.

"Friend"raising, or gathering allies and supporters, is an important concept that may make achieving positive outcomes a little easier. Political candidates and elected officials are often very good at putting this theory into practice. Gifted politicians can recite the name and a related fact about people who have donated or volunteered for them in the past. The same should hold true for us. If we want people to continue sharing their service with us, we must commend them for their work and make sure they feel truly appreciated. People want to be part of a winning team and hope to be inspired along the way. If you can do both of these things while making others feel supported and stimulated you will be able to "friend"raise with the best.

When you are raising funds for your church, non-profit group, or even a charity run or walk, you want to be able to reach out to friends who will be able to either give of their sweat equity or financial resources. Having a large possible donor or volunteer base that is easily accessible and organized is essential when you are trying to motivate your peers to assist you. It is a good

Thoughts for Leaders:

"My friends are my estate."

Emily Dickinson

idea to keep in touch with others through as many mechanisms as possible. For a former colleague or classmate it is not far fetched to have saved their email address, phone number, and home address while also being connected to them through social networking sites like Facebook, MySpace, and LinkedIn. The more ways that you are able to alert others to what you are working on, the better off you will be in the long run.

Think about a few specific ways in which you can "friend"raise today. Consider organizing a holiday card list, asking a few old classmates to be your friends on Facebook, or giving a call to a colleague you haven't spoken with in awhile. This "friend"raising will pay off in the long run, possibly through donations, job referrals, or even just having a free place to stay when you visit a new city. Managing professional and personal relationships is important business that we all must dedicate some time to regularly if we hope to bring our team with us on our leadership journey.

Unleash Your Creative Side

My friend Harry and I recently attended a playoff hockey game. As we were walking into the arena, Harry turned to me and said, "I need you to come into the bathroom and paint me." To which I appropriately responded, "What are you talking about?!?" Harry decided that he wanted to paint himself black and gold to show his support for our hometown team and needed my help. While I found the visual of two men pushing 30 years old in a bathroom with paint a little odd, I decided I would assist him. Harry had a great time and even got some camera time on the jumbotron. I give him a lot of credit for being creative and trying to do something to entertain others and make them smile. We all have friends like Harry. They are the people who sing at karaoke night, don't mind talking to complete strangers, or volunteer to participate in games and contests at events. These people showcase the fact that we shouldn't take ourselves too seriously and should enjoy new and unique experiences.

If you haven't tried to do something outside of the box recently, I would encourage you to do so soon. I love movies and have a frighteningly large collection of DVDs and even VHS tapes.

Due to this, I have always been curious about how movies are made and what a set feels and looks like. A few months ago I decided to accept an opportunity to be a paid extra in a movie filming in my city and even got selected to dress as a pilot. While the experience wasn't as glamorous as I had hoped, I am definitely glad I gave it a chance and have been able to share some fun stories with my friends. I hope that you will undertake a similar unique opportunity in your own life.

Thoughts for Leaders:

"Don't fear failure so much that you refuse to try new things. The saddest summary of a life contains three descriptions: could have, might have, and should have."

Louis E. Boone

What is something that you have always been interested in doing but have never attempted? Some possibilities include, but certainly aren't limited to: playing an instrument, writing poetry, taking a dance or acting class, trying out a new sport or hobby, or visiting a museum or theater that was previously off your radar. I had a great time recently dragon boat racing. This is definitely not something I had ever sought out to do, but had a really fun time experiencing it. Schedule time and make plans to get outside of your comfort zone and try new and creative things in the upcoming weeks. No matter what happens, you will have some great stories to share at work the next day and hopefully will unleash some creative energy.

Why Not You?

One of my favorite motivators is the always energized Donny Deutsch, host of The Big Idea on CNBC. Deutsch made millions running Deutsch Inc. and now hosts his show as a way to inspire business-minded professionals as he aims to enable others to capture the American Dream. In Deutsch's book "Often Wrong, Never in Doubt" Deutsch shares the sentiment of "why not me", which has become one of my favorite thoughts to share with the groups that I speak to.

The concept of asking yourself "why not me" is so simple but is also very important. We should all question ourselves about why we shouldn't be the new chair or president of an organization. The same holds true with other opportunities including starting a business, planning new events, expressing interest in a promotion, or any other possible significant undertakings in your life. If you don't stick your neck out there it is likely that someone else will. There always will be people who are willing to dream big and try new things. Why shouldn't you be one of those leaders and innovators?

Your kitchen cabinet, as it is often referred to within politics, is a collection of your closest friends and family who serve as advisors regarding the big decisions in your life. It is probable that this circle of friends might shoot down some ideas that you have when you are thinking "why not me" about new experiences and opportunities. While it is vital to listen to their counsel and not act in a reckless manner, it is just as important to think big and try to achieve and make a difference in a meaningful way. By

Thoughts for Leaders:

"The key to success is not purely who's the smartest, who's the best, but also who can say with conviction, 'I deserve it.' The entire concept is wrapped up in one phrase: 'Why not me?'."

Donny Deutsch

passing over opportunities, the likelihood increases that you will find yourself Monday morning quarterbacking about recent oversights. If you believe in yourself and express why it should be you, others will rally around you with passion and enthusiasm. The next time that you find yourself over thinking a decision, make sure to ask yourself, why not me!

Why Not You?

What are four big opportunities that you have recently considered and either put on the backburner or passed over?

1. _____

2. _____

3. _____

4. _____

Please take some time and determine how you can make your move regarding each of these decisions. Strive to tackle one of these challenges today. You won't regret it!

Why Should You Get Involved?

The reasons why people decide to get involved differ greatly. Since we are all driven by our own unique motivating factors and forces it makes sense that we are led to join groups in a diverse set of ways. Some of the most common reasons others have shared with me for getting involved are to make a difference, meet new people, stay busy, strengthen their resume, and develop connections. Often times, it is also a specific cause, event, or group that will motivate someone to become more engaged in their community. My hope is that people who become passionate for a specific reason will continue to extend their commitment to other organizations that can benefit from their expertise and service.

There are personal and professional benefits to making a difference as a leader. These include increased communication skills, teamwork, leadership, moral development, crisis management skills, event planning, and even better mental health and self esteem. Being active also allows us to meet and work with people from different backgrounds and gain new important perspectives. These experiences strengthen our core values and give us a better sense of social responsibility.

Getting involved truly has made my life so much better. I was an unhappy and somewhat lost ninth grader when I made a commitment to being a leader through clubs and organizations. Up until my early high school years I had always assumed I would be a professional baseball player when I grew up. It was definitely a naïve assumption but I truly believed it. My skill level

Thoughts for Leaders:

"It is hard to fail, but it is worse never to have tried to succeed."

Theodore Roosevelt

began to decrease a bit at the exact same time that my passion for sports journalism elevated greatly. I really leaped into the school newspaper and it set me on a journey of organizational involvement which has continued for the last 15 years. I often credit our newspaper advisor at my high school, Angela Mazza, for being the person who opened my eyes to experiences beyond baseball and for believing that I could do more than just hit the long ball. She was an important mentor who impacted my life and got me moving in a positive direction.

I hope that you decide to do more as a result of reading this book and am a firm believer that we can all try one new thing or undertake one new responsibility in our lives. Within my own life I find that the busier I am, the more productive and energetic I tend to feel. The day also goes quicker when there is a board meeting, sports game, or event to attend that evening. Getting involved should be fun! If you are not having a good time through these involvements, then you most likely have not found the right fit quite yet. Keep going out and tackling new challenges and undertaking new initiatives. You will grow personally and professionally, gain valuable transferable skills, and have a good time along the way.

Share Your Story

I really hope that this book has encouraged you to do something positive outside of work, school, or your other daily routines. In this book, I got the chance to share with you some tips, thoughts,

Thoughts for Leaders:

"You must get involved to have an impact. No one is impressed with the won-lost record of the referee."

Napoleon Hill

experiences, and stories that I hope made a lasting impression on you. Now it is your turn. Please visit www.bakerleadership.com and contact me to let me know what you are doing to make a difference. Tell me about the committees that you have joined, the fundraisers that you have attended, or the groups that you have started. No matter how small you may think it is, I am curious to hear what you are doing and how you are getting involved.

I feel strongly that our generation needs to step up and do more to improve our communities, schools, places of worship, recreation centers, senior centers, food banks, and other places that impact our fellow citizens. Do not let your 20s and 30s escape you without making an impact in all that you do. Let's all change the world together - starting today!

ABOUT THE AUTHOR

Tom Baker is the President of Baker Leadership, the Executive Director of Healthy Teens, Inc., and President of the Pittsburgh Urban Magnet Project (PUMP). His previous professional experience includes serving as a Family Recruiter at Three Rivers Adoption Council, as a Career Counselor at Carnegie Mellon University's H. John Heinz III School of Public Policy and Management, and as Director of The Learning Ladder Child Development Center in Lancaster, PA. Tom has served on a number of boards for non-profit organizations including PUMP (President), Greenfield Organization, Pittsburgh Cares, Life Span, Inc.(Secretary), Pittsburgh Singles Volunteer Network (Vice President), and National Student Partnerships (Chairman). He was Student Body President and President of Lambda Chi Alpha while earning his Bachelors degree in Elementary Education from Millersville University and served as President of the Associates for Student Development during his graduate studies in Student Affairs in Higher Education at Indiana University of PA. Tom is a proud member of Homestead-Amity-McCandless Lodge 582 of Free and Accepted Masons, the Monroeville Rotary Club, and lives with his wife, Erin, in Pittsburgh, PA.

RESERVE YOUR COPY TODAY!

Buy the book that's inspiring a generation to *Get Involved* and make the most of their 20s and 30s!

Author Tom Baker's book motivates with descriptions of countless ways you can make a difference.

There is something for everyone in this unique and powerful book. Find out how you can change the world!

visit **www.bakerleadership.com** for more information

FREE SHIPPING on all orders!

Please detach and return with your payment to: Baker Leadership, PO Box 81566, Pittsburgh, PA 15217

Name: _____

Shipping Address: _____

Email: _____ Phone: _____

Number of copies ordered: _____ Total Price ($15 each): _____

Please circle one: CHECK   CASH

Check Number: _____

Please visit www.bakerleadership.com to purchase with a credit card.